The Bakerl

M. A. C. Horne

UNDERGROUND

Capital Transport

First published 2001

ISBN 185414 248 8

Published in association with London's Transport Museum
by Capital Transport Publishing, 38 Long Elmes, Harrow Weald, Middlesex

Printed by CS Graphics, Singapore

CONTENTS

WAVING 1/6

BAKERLOO!
TUBE

ATION

OXFORD
STREET

·OX

KER

ALBER

BAKERLOO TUBE

THE NORTH AND SOUTH ROUTE
THROUGH THE WEST END.

CONNECTIONS WITH ALL PARTS.

From this Station

TO

	IN MINS
PICCADILLY CIRCUS	2
For Piccadilly Tube for Hammersmith, Knightsbridge Holborn, Kings X Etc.	
TRAFALGAR SQUARE	4
for S E & C Ry	
EMBANKMENT (Charing X)	5
For District Ry for Sloane Square, Victoria Temple, Blackfriars Etc.	
WATERLOO For L & S W Ry	7
WESTMINSTER BRIDGE ROAD	9
ELEPHANT & CASTLE	11
for C & S L Ry for Oval Stockwell Clapham Common London Bridge Etc. LCC Trams for South London Districts S E & C Ry for Crystal Palace Etc.	
REGENT'S PARK for Zoo	2
BAKER STREET	4
for Met Ry St Johns Wood Lord Etc	
GREAT CENTRAL	5
for Great Central Ry & Metrop	
EDGWARE Rd.	7

THROUGH BOOKINGS — SEASON TICKETS

Origins and Construction

The Bakerloo Line is a product of the early Edwardian boom in tube railway construction. The 6.7 miles (10.7km) from Elephant & Castle to Queen's Park is nearly all within the Underground's familiar deep-level tube environment, but the remaining 7.7 miles (12.3km) to Harrow & Wealdstone operates over Railtrack's metals, with services shared with Silverlink's Watford local service; the Bakerloo itself used to serve Watford Junction. For much of its life the Bakerloo Line also served the Middlesex suburbs of Willesden Green, Wembley Park and Stanmore by means of a branch diverging at Baker Street. However, in 1979 the Stanmore branch was transferred to the then new Jubilee Line, and its tube history is covered in more detail in the Jubilee Line book.

Even in early Victorian times the construction of conventional railways in central London was considered very undesirable, if not impracticable. That didn't stop aspirations from forming. One such wish was for an underground railway link between the north side of the River Thames and the inconveniently situated London terminus of the London & South Western Railway (LSWR) at Waterloo, a concept beset with difficulty for nearly 40 years. An early scheme was the Waterloo & Whitehall Railway, which dated back to 1865. This was intended to run between Great Scotland Yard

Map showing the route of the Bakerloo Railway across London portraying the unopened (and partly unbuilt) extension to Paddington.

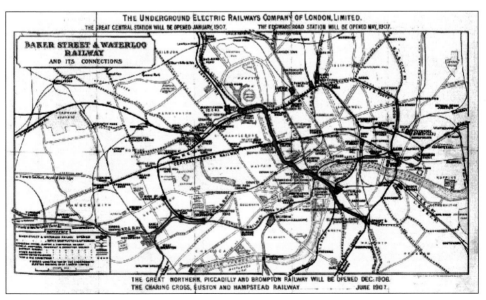

(near Charing Cross) and Waterloo station, and was interesting in that it reflected an early desire to put a city-centre railway beneath the street in relatively small sized tunnels and beneath the River Thames in wrought iron tubes. Electric traction had not yet been developed, and to propel the trains pneumatic power was proposed, avoiding the need for steam locomotives. This system followed promising results obtained from experimental work for a mail-conveying pneumatic railway built between Euston and Holborn (opened in 1865). Here the carriages were fitted with a flexible flange that prevented air from passing the carriage in the tunnel. A difference between the air pressures in the tunnel either side of the carriage would therefore cause it to move. The system was a technical success, if not a commercial one.

A considerable amount of construction was undertaken on the Waterloo & Whitehall scheme, but an untimely financial crisis in 1866 made it impossible to raise the additional capital needed to complete the work. With cash lacking the company could not survive and its fate was sealed, although its formal demise was not until 1882. The opening of the South Eastern Railway's station at Waterloo in 1869 (linking the area with Charing Cross) also diminished the immediate need for another cross-river railway on a similar route.

A later proposal was known as the Charing Cross & Waterloo Electric Railway, which obtained an Act of Incorporation in August 1882. This was a cut-and-cover scheme although the line beneath the river was to be carried in twin iron caissons lowered into a trench – similar to the Waterloo & Whitehall proposal. The northern terminus was to be near Trafalgar Square, while the southern one was intended underneath the LSWR's Waterloo station, some five-eighths of a mile away (1 km). The enabling Act provided for first, second and third class passengers (at maximum fares of sixpence, fourpence and threepence respectively). With Dr C.W. Siemens as its electrical engineer this might well have emerged as the first electric underground railway in London, but adequate finance was not forthcoming and almost no construction work was undertaken, the company becoming defunct by a further Act of 1885. Siemens's death in 1883 must have been a severe blow to the company.

The Baker Street & Waterloo Railway (BS&WR) was a more ambitious scheme. The first evidence of moves to provide a railway between these two points emerged in 1891 when an attempt was made to promote a Bill in Parliament. In addition to the now familiar Charing Cross – Waterloo link, which formed the southern end of the proposal, it was to continue northwards to upper Baker Street. This alignment would considerably improve north-south communication across central London, and this factor was reflected in the first prospective name of the concern – the North & South London Railway. The 3-mile line was to have been constructed in twin iron-lined tube tunnels, the success of this method having been proved by the City & South London Railway which had opened in 1890 as the first electric tube railway in the world. It is said that the original spur for the line was the desire for businessmen in the Westminster area to be able to get to Lords to see the end of the day's play, but that such a route, upon examination, demonstrated that even wider benefits were possible, and the line could perhaps be very profitable.

Under its revised name, the BS&WR was eventually incorporated by an Act of Parliament of 28th March 1893. The extremities of the route were described as New Street (now Melcombe Street) near upper Baker Street, to the southern side of James Street, near Lower Marsh at its Waterloo end. In common with certain other early tube schemes the carriage of both first and second-class passengers was allowed for, at maximum rates of twopence or threepence a mile respectively. The carriage of mails

The main worksite for the Bakerloo was built on temporary staging in the Thames. This photo shows the not inconsiderable facilities that were provided.

and small parcels was catered for, but goods traffic was prohibited. A number of 'parliamentary' trains, calling at all stations, was required at the usual penny a mile rate. Raising the finance again proved to be a major obstacle and the company lay virtually dormant for some years.

The BS&WR remained optimistic about overcoming its financial difficulties and obtained a second Act of Parliament in 1896; this authorised an extension of time, a further increase in capital, and an almost quarter-mile projection beneath New Street and Melcombe Place to the Marylebone station of the Great Central Railway, then under construction; this new station was not otherwise conveniently served by underground railways. Although two of the BS&WR's board were also directors of the LSWR the latter company were disinclined to offer financial assistance to the tube company, evidently believing that the feeder traffic likely to be generated did not warrant the (considerable) outlay. It must be said that at the time the LSWR were embroiled in their own scheme to build an underground railway, but their objective was the City – the Waterloo & City Railway opened in 1898.

In the event help came from the direction of a mining finance company, repeating the Central London Railway's experience in 1895. This time it was the London & Globe Finance Corporation which came to the rescue, and a contract was signed between the two concerns on 4th November 1897. In due course the BS&WR board was replaced by one identical to that of the London & Globe. The company was one of several of which a certain Whitaker Wright was in sole effective control. Wright, though an Englishman, had made his fortune in the United States in mine prospecting, and on his return to his native country lived in mildly eccentric affluence. He set up business in the City, and gradually spawned a network of companies, many of which were involved in financing mining. His companies were characterised by the existence on their boards of various dignitaries of whom few, if any, took part in their activities.

The London & Globe became the main contractor for the new railway and took upon itself the responsibility for bringing the new line into being. The construction of the tunnels was subcontracted to Perry & Company. Work began in August 1898 from a staging on the River Thames near Hungerford Bridge, from which point two shafts were sunk. The river staging avoided the need to find suitable land sites in central London while allowing for removal of spoil and delivery of materials by barge. Amongst

Constructing the tunnels involved bringing in vast quantities of heavy materials, as well as removal of spoil. The first tubes used pit ponies, but the Bakerloo was able to avail itself of small electric locomotives supplied by temporary overhead line.

other facilities provided on the staging were various workshops and a small generating station for temporary power and lighting in the tunnels. The twin running tunnels, of 11ft 8¼ins (3.56m) diameter, were to be driven both north and south from the bottom of these shafts, together with additional shafts along the line of route. All tunnels were to be driven by hydraulically powered 'Greathead' tunnelling shields, successfully used on the City & South London. Stations were to be situated at: Waterloo (beneath the LSWR station), Charing Cross (beneath the District Railway station), Trafalgar Square, Piccadilly Circus, Oxford Circus, Baker Street and Marylebone.

A further extension of time was granted by a third Act of Parliament, of August 1899, by which time the company had expended some £300,000. This Act also authorised the southern end of the line to deviate slightly westwards to terminate at the south-east end of Addington Street, allowing for an improved arrangement at the depot and power station (the original site having been in Lower Marsh). Also authorised were subways from the ticket hall area at Trafalgar Square station leading to various nearby street corners.

In 1900 further reflections required the BS&WR to obtain a fourth Act of Parliament, authorising two further extensions. At the northern end a route was sanctioned from Marylebone to Paddington (Great Western Railway) station, near the junction of Bishops Road and Gloucester Terrace; an intermediate station was visualised at Edgware Road, apparently on the western side. It was perhaps for the best that a proposal was thrown out at the bill stage to build a branch line from a point north of Oxford Circus to Euston; it took the Victoria Line to acknowledge the usefulness of such a link when it opened in 1969.

At the southern end of the line the company was authorised to project beyond Waterloo to the busy Elephant & Castle road intersection (with subway connection to the nearby City & South London Railway station) – this nearly mile-long extension terminated in the New Kent Road. The company was to construct the Elephant & Castle ticket hall beneath the road junction itself, with subway entrances from the various street corners. In addition to these the 1900 Act authorised a different depot and power station site near St George's Circus, Southwark, and the construction of a 650-yard link from the depot to the main BS&WR route. When work began, the subcontract for the northern extension went to Perry & Company, while that for the depot and Elephant & Castle extension went to John Mowlem.

But the London & Globe was not all it appeared to be, and when some of Wright's ventures sustained heavy losses a number of financial irregularities came to light – these showed several 'successful' companies to be in severe trouble. At the close of 1900 the London & Globe and some associated companies announced their insolvency, the crash dragging down in its wake numerous firms of stockbrokers. Wright maintained his composure until the end of 1901 when he was subjected to what was called at the time a public examination. His exposure as a potential fraud encouraged him to withdraw to Paris.

The majesty of the law was characteristically slow in its pursuit of justice but was hastened by angry creditors who short-circuited the inaction of the Attorney General. As soon as the intention to prosecute was known, Wright attempted to flee to the United States – he was arrested upon arrival and in due course extradited back to London where he was successfully prosecuted for publishing false balance sheets and accounts. The case would have been heard at the Old Bailey but for an application by Wright's counsel to have it heard at the Royal Courts of Justice under civil rather than criminal procedure. This re-arrangement allowed Wright his final opportunity to cheat his fellows. Had he been convicted at the Old Bailey then police procedures would have been followed and immediate imprisonment was ensured. At the Law Courts matters were dealt with rather differently and Wright was allowed to consult his advisors unsupervised in a private room. He eluded his seven-year prison sentence by means of a cyanide capsule, and it was with considerable embarrassment that upon his body was found not only a second capsule but also a revolver, which he had evidently had in court with him. Upon such characters did the future development of the London Underground depend!

Against this colourful and intriguing background the BS&WR had been partially built, representing some of the more solid assets of the London & Globe. Substantial progress had been made on the running tunnels and on a few of the station tunnels, and some work on the depot site had been started. But the collapse of the financial backing caused activity to be scaled down drastically, and throughout 1901 much of the railway workings became virtually moribund. A little money trickled in from share calls from non-institutional shareholders, and on a monthly basis the BS&WR paid the sub-contractors directly for the small amount of work pushed ahead, mainly between the river and Oxford Circus.

By August 1901 the state of affairs was as follows. The southbound tunnel was complete from the river shaft to a point 90 yards southwards (this required working in compressed air). North of the river shaft the same tunnel had just been completed as far as Regent Street, just north of Conduit Street. The station tunnels had been bored at Embankment, Trafalgar Square and Piccadilly Circus. The northbound tunnel was complete from the Waterloo station tunnel (of which 20 yards had been excavated) to a point in Regent Street 107 yards north of Vigo Street, where work had been suspended on 4th May 1901. The station tunnels had been dug at Trafalgar Square and Piccadilly Circus, but at Embankment a small-bore tunnel had been driven through the

Bakerloo station tunnel under construction. LT Museum

station site and the tunnel still required enlarging. From the same date work had been suspended on the tunnel drives southwards from Baker Street, the southbound tunnel having reached a point near Park Square, and the northbound tunnel extending to Portland Place, just south of Park Crescent. It would appear that one station tunnel was complete at Baker Street while the other required opening out from temporary running tunnel, built to expedite progress.

While the construction of the railway had been progressing, there were others who had been taking an interest in London's public transport affairs. Prior to the Globe's collapse at the end of 1900 negotiations had already been taking place with an American syndicate headed by Albert L. Johnson with a view to its taking over the Baker Street & Waterloo interests; presumably the ailing Globe would have been grateful to exchange its long-term interests in the railway for hard cash. The negotiations were never completed, apparently being pre-empted by events. (Johnson was involved in the American tramroad industry and appears to have come to London in 1899 to promote an electric railway from London to Brighton. He died in Brooklyn in July 1901). It was another American who came to the railway's rescue after the Globe had sunk. This time the man was Charles Tyson Yerkes, who had made his particular fortune in Philadelphia and Chicago by building and improving city transport, especially by modernising and electrifying existing old-fashioned systems. He did this with no lack of criticism, especially of his motives. His forte was to carry out property speculation in areas likely to benefit from any improved transport services. It had been suggested to him that London offered similar opportunities and so it happened that Yerkes became interested in London's transport difficulties. By 1900 his syndicate had acquired the steam-hauled Metropolitan District Railway (MDR) and several unrelated tube railway schemes. The former he intended to electrify and completely re-equip;

10

the latter he intended to construct from new. Agreement between the Baker Street & Waterloo, the Globe's liquidators and Yerkes's Metropolitan District Electric Traction Company was reached in March 1902, and the future of the tube scheme was secured.

As Yerkes's aspirations grew a larger and more flexible company was required to handle the increasingly complex arrangements needed. The vehicle emerged in 1902 as the Underground Electric Railways Company of London Limited (UERL), and this took overall control of his various tube schemes as well as the MDR and the Traction company. The UERL was to run much of London's transport for the next 31 years. In addition to the BS&WR, two other tubes emerged under the Yerkes banner, though Yerkes's death in 1905 meant he never saw them in operation. The other companies were the Great Northern, Piccadilly & Brompton Railway (GNP&BR) and the Charing Cross, Euston & Hampstead Railway (CCE&HR). These cumbersome titles were soon shortened to Piccadilly Tube and Hampstead Tube in the eyes of the public, and were later to form trunk sections of what are now (respectively) the Piccadilly and Northern Lines. Whatever Yerkes's original motives may have been – of which there is much speculation – there is no doubt that his drive, commitment and money built or transformed London's underground railways and there must be grave doubts whether anything on that scale would have happened otherwise.

The UERL was appointed the main contractor for all three Yerkes tube railways and so far as possible similar standards and styles were adopted. The BS&WR differed from its two compatriots in that a substantial amount had already been built and it was extremely difficult to adapt some of this work to suit the new (and higher) standard. Thus BS&WR platforms were shorter than on the other two lines, and the layouts of the partly constructed stations were somewhat awkward. Indeed the layout at Oxford Circus was so objectionable that the UERL desired to make some alterations. By this time the Board of Trade (responsible for approving the designs) had itself set higher standards of access and safety for new construction and took the opportunity to protest at the arrangements at Oxford Circus. This resulted in major reconstruction of the low-level passages, and gives Oxford Circus the unusual privilege of being the only tube station to be substantially rebuilt before it even opened.

The BS&WR's fifth Act (in 1902) further extended the authorised time for completing the railway, and noted in the preamble that £944,702 had so far been expended and the railway was largely complete from Waterloo to Oxford Circus. In 1903 another Act authorised the taking of additional lands near Lambeth Christ Church, and also allowed the company to make an agreement with the UERL for the supply of electricity (avoiding the need for the BS&WR to build its own power station at the St George's Circus depot, better known as London Road depot). A second Act of 1903 further extended the railway's time to complete the works.

By March 1903 some 80 per cent of the running tunnels were complete from Waterloo to Dorset Square and all authorised station tunnels were complete on that section, except for one platform at Waterloo. Little work had been undertaken south of Waterloo but contractors had just begun operations on the future depot site. It was another year before the running tunnels north of Waterloo were complete, apart from the crossover north of Baker Street; work was also in progress on equipping some of the stations. South of Waterloo about a quarter of the depot excavation had been undertaken and good progress was being made on the running tunnels.

In 1904 yet another Act authorised construction of two additional stations, one at Kennington Road (now Lambeth North) and the other at Regent's Park. The tunnelling was well advanced and this necessitated the new station tunnels being constructed from around the existing running tunnels. The Act also provided powers to construct a station at Edgware Road on the Paddington extension; the building was to be on the eastern side of that road (on the corner of Bell Street) superseding the earlier thoughts for a station on the other side. Here, the running tunnels were not yet started and the station could be built conventionally. The opportunity was also taken to require the BS&WR to build a conventional station building at Elephant & Castle, instead of a booking hall beneath the road.

By July 1904 platforms were being installed at several stations and most of the low-level subway works were nearly complete. South of Waterloo good progress was being made with tunnelling and with excavation of the depot site. Work on the Edgware Road extension had also begun. Early in 1905 the tunnels were complete from Elephant & Castle to Baker Street except for a short stretch at Elephant & Castle; about half the track had also been laid. Some of the station superstructures had been started, platform installation continued with some tiling work now under way. About a third of the depot site remained unexcavated but work on erecting some of the buildings had begun. The electrical work had started, as had preparation for the lifts. The rolling stock was also on order.

Towards the end of 1905 the line had largely taken shape and much of the rolling stock had already been delivered to the depot. When the railway had been promoted, trains hauled by locomotives had been contemplated. This method was already in use on the City & South London Railway, and the lessons learned there had been adopted by the Central London (opened in 1900), who had ordered more powerful locomotives and more robust electrical equipment. But the delay in the BS&WR's construction meant that a new and apparently better technology were now available – multiple unit operation. With this, the motors and electrical equipment were distributed throughout the train, so no locomotives were required (simplifying operation and avoiding the vibration problems which dogged the Central London until it switched to multiple units in 1903).

Three types of carriage were now required, though the American term 'car' quickly came into vogue and has stayed since; there were 36 cars of each type. The motor cars had a driving cab at one end and at the other was a gated entrance platform allowing access to the car interior through end doors. Trailer cars had no motors or equipment compartments and had gated platforms at both ends; control trailers were similar but had drivers' control equipment mounted on one of the gated platforms. The car exteriors were finished in a red livery with cream upper panels.

The Bakerloo cars were actually built in America and shipped to the UK partially dismantled. This photograph appears to show a complete car erected at the car builders for demonstration purposes, complete with an Americanised version of the Bakerloo's name. ACF's Berwick plant (Pennsylvania) was the first of theirs to specialise in steel construction and had already supplied cars to New York's system.

The cars for the Bakerloo, erected at Trafford Park, were hauled to Camden Town on their own wheels by the London & North Western Railway. The placard on the side of the first car reads: 'Electric Car Train, conveyed by L&NWR'.

The 108 cars were built in the USA by the American Car & Foundry Company and shipped in a dismantled state to Trafford Park in Manchester. Here they were assembled and marshalled into trains which were then conveyed by the London & North Western Railway to Camden goods depot. Individual cars were then put onto road 'bogies' and hauled (generally using horses) through central London each night to London Road depot. Here they had to carefully negotiate the sharp turn and steep gradient into the yard; this was not always accomplished without incident, and early morning tram services were sometimes held up severely. The first car arrived on 12th September 1905.

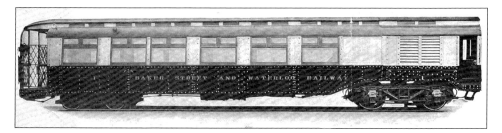

Above One of the original Bakerloo motor cars in its as-delivered livery. Passengers entered the car from the gated end (left) through the end door. The driving cab (right) was next to the motor bogie, which the underframe was carried over to clear. Trailer cars had a gated entrance at both ends. The blank panel over the motor bogie was finished as a 'blind' window. Retouching artists often adjusted this to make it look like a genuine window, as in the view below.

Left Bakerloo car equipped with 'road bogies' ready for haulage through the streets.

View of Baker Street station around opening date. This was one of the larger stations on the Bakerloo.

Interior of Bakerloo Line carriage as delivered in 1906. In anticipation of standing passengers (not quickly realised) strap handles were provided. The Spartan appearance was soon to be cheered up by the introduction of advertising.

View of the depot at London Road still under construction, but with some cars already delivered.

The outlet from the depot was equipped with its own signal cabin (above the entrance to the tunnels). The right hand tunnel leads to a shunting neck, the left hand one towards Waterloo.

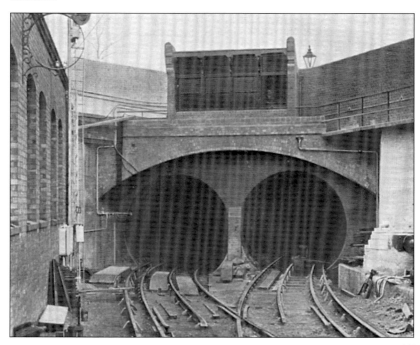

Open for Business

The central portion of the new tube was ready for opening early in 1906, and for several weeks a full service of empty trains was operated to train and acclimatise the staff. The big day was Saturday 10th March. The opening ceremony was performed by the Chairman of the London County Council, Sir Edwin Cornwall MP, after which the line was heavily patronised for the remainder of the day. At this stage the service operated only between Baker Street and Kennington Road.

The company name 'Baker Street & Waterloo Railway' was far too cumbersome for everyday use by Londoners, who sought something snappier; the cheaper newspapers inevitably rallied to the cause. The *Evening News* referred to the tube as the "Baker-loo" in one of its headlines; the name had a certain ring about it and despite adverse comment elsewhere the company itself soon started to use it, the hyphen soon being dropped. Fortunately suggestions from some other papers (*The Star* referred to the line as "the 'Loo") were ignored. The word 'Tube' was much bandied about at the time, too, and the various underground railways also latched onto that. However, after only a little while the epithet 'tube' was officially suppressed by the Yerkes lines in favour of 'Underground' or 'Railway', as appropriate. But 'Bakerloo' stuck, and is, of course, the name still with us today. The exact inventor of 'Bakerloo' is not easily discernible, but an obituary in the *News Chronicle* for 27th May 1933 attributes it to Captain G.H.F. Nichols who began his Fleet Street career as a reporter on the *Evening News* (though, intriguingly, not until a year after the line had opened using the Bakerloo name). It remains a mystery.

However promising interest in the line may have been on the opening day, traffic during the following few weeks was extremely disappointing and was a matter of some initial concern. To reduce unnecessary cost, train lengths were substantially reduced. It did not bode well for the other two Yerkes lines, which had not yet opened. Fortunately matters improved after a few months and the railway soon established itself as the vital link its promoters envisaged. A factor in this may have been the abandonment in July 1906 of charging a flat fare of twopence in favour of a charge relating to distance – fares then varied between a penny and threepence in halfpenny steps.

Notwithstanding the slow beginning, the public found a soundly built railway constructed to high standards of comfort, safety and convenience, and noticeably better than the other deep-level tubes which were in existence at that time.

Station buildings were of a standard general design used throughout the three UERL tubes though adapted to the requirements of individual sites. Designed by Leslie W. Green, each station was a two-storey structure clothed in ruby red glazed

Trafalgar Square station had a below ground ticket hall beneath the square itself. This photograph shows one of the three stairwells; this one emerges within the Square, and the other two on the corner of Strand and the eastern side of the Square. Morley's Hotel (opposite) was later replaced by South Africa House. Note that Paddington has been included on the sign but covered over, dating the sign as pre-1913. LT Museum terracotta. At Regent's Park and Trafalgar Square stations it was not possible to construct surface buildings, so entirely below-ground ticket halls had to be built; access from the street was via steps and subways. At Charing Cross, which the BS&WR confusingly called Embankment, access to the tube railway was gained by means of a long inclined subway leading down from the existing MDR Charing Cross station, and no separate station building was constructed. Over the river, at Waterloo, much work had already been completed before Leslie Green's designs emerged, and the ticket hall reflected earlier plans, though finishings to an entrance in York Road did reflect Green's style.

At platform level it seems the decor originally planned would have followed the practice of the City & South and Central London Railways, with glazed white tiling covering the entire platform tunnel vault, maximising the reflection of precious lighting. Tiling work on this theme was started by early 1904 at Trafalgar Square. But while this was going on Yerkes appears to have taken a personal interest in the platform finishings, which resulted in experimental finishes at another station, probably Waterloo. The result was a patterned tiling scheme devised for each station; again the patterns follow a theme but gives each station on all three Yerkes lines a unique colour/pattern combination. The designs are generally attributed to Leslie Green and on the whole were favourably reviewed in the press. The concept perhaps echoed the designs of New York subway stations where different patterns were used at each station – it is said to be an attempt to assist those who couldn't read to work out where they were by recognising the patterns.

Except at Charing Cross, communication between the surface and lower stations

Trafalgar Square station just before opening. This style was entirely typical of most stations. Most of the lighting was provided by centrally suspended arc lamps, with filament lamps as backup.

was by means of lifts, between two and four at each location in either one or two shafts (often the original working shafts). Each lift could accommodate between 50 and 70 people, plus the lift operator, and all were provided by the Otis Elevator Company (another American firm). The winding gear was accommodated on the first floor level of the stations, but at Trafalgar Square and Regents Park the equipment had to be placed at the bottom of the shafts. All the lift stations also had a smaller shaft containing a spiral staircase for emergency use. Entry gates to the lifts were hand-operated by the lift attendants (who also checked tickets), but another Underground first was the remote operation of the exit gates by compressed air, the lift attendant operating a lever by the entrance. All this meant it was possible for people to leave the lifts by the gates opposite to those used for entry, maintaining a one-way flow which, as far as possible, was maintained throughout the station passageways.

In order for electricity to be taken from the UERL's central generating station at Lots Road (near Chelsea Creek) it was necessary for high tension feeder cables to be brought to a substation and distribution point at Charing Cross (above the BS&WR's station), from which point power was distributed to the railway's other two substations at London Road and Baker Street. Current was supplied to the trains via two conductor rails (one between the running rails and the other outside) at around 600 volts dc. Evidence of current leakage between the outer conductor rail and the tunnels initially caused the positive rail to be in the centre and the negative rail outside, but the situation was reversed in 1917 when inter-running with other systems began. As a safety precaution telephone wires were provided throughout the tunnels so that a motorman (as the drivers were called) could quickly speak to the adjacent stations to get the power turned off, or summon other help, in an emergency; each train carried portable telephone handsets which could be clipped to the wires for this purpose. (About 20 years later the system had been modified so that clipping the telephone to the wires, or touching the wires together, would discharge current automatically.)

Signalling was substantially automatic, using a system already tried in America and designed by Westinghouse (a similar system was successfully used on the Metropolitan District Railway from 1905). This used electrically energised track circuits, which operated the signals; these consisted of pneumatically controlled spectacle plates moved to show the appropriate coloured light. At each stop signal a pneumatically controlled lever next to the running rails, called a 'trainstop', was raised when a red aspect was shown; this was designed to engage with a 'tripcock' on a passing train and thus apply the emergency brakes. At the stations where there were crossovers the signals were semi-automatic and were under the overriding control of a signalman. Both signals and points were fully interlocked and controlled from a miniature lever frame, the signalman establishing the position of trains from an illuminated track diagram (there were locations where he couldn't physically see the trains at all). Signal cabins were therefore provided initially at Kennington Road, London Road Depot, and at the crossover west of Baker Street, about which something now needs to be said.

Although the initial passenger service terminated at Baker Street this had not been envisaged as a permanent terminus and the platforms and tracks were on different levels, making the provision of a crossover there awkward. Trains had therefore to carry on beyond, to reverse along the Paddington extension, which had still not been finished. Fortunately there was a crossover tunnel east of Marylebone and the empty trains had to run just beyond this to reverse in the northbound tunnel. As Marylebone station was incomplete a temporary signal cabin had to be built, actually in the crossover tunnel itself, over the tracks.

Although the works at Marylebone and Edgware Road were still unfinished, the final section – to Paddington – hadn't actually been started. Plans for what to do at the north-western end of the line could not be settled, and went through several major revisions. It was clear that Paddington main line terminus was a very important traffic objective, but the issue was where to head after that; the geography meant that future aspirations were critically linked to the general alignment by which Paddington was approached.

The authorised alignment was historical. Paddington BS&WR station had been intended to be near Bishops Bridge Road, connecting with the Great Western station by means of a long subway beneath Eastbourne Terrace. This arrangement was made in contemplation of an 1899 scheme to extend the BS&WR to Royal Oak, and thence to Willesden on the London & North Western Railway. In the event it was decided not to seek powers for the portion west of Paddington in what became the company's 1900 Act. The long interchange passage to the GWR would have been far from ideal and with the looming financial crisis and then the hiatus of new ownership there was no rush to start something that deserved further detailed examination.

After some delay, a start on the extension was made as far as Edgware Road, with Paddington intended to follow on as soon as all the issues had been gone into. In the event a more satisfactory scheme was not planned and authorised until the railway's 1906 Act. This was for a shorter route, deviating from the earlier one just west of Edgware Road station (which of course was now partly constructed). Whilst this brought the tube nearer to the main line station at Paddington, and provided for a good interchange with the other existing railways, the BS&WR would have terminated under the corner of Devonport Street and Grand Junction Road pointing due south-east. The disadvantage was the awkwardness of future extension in the direction ripest for it, north-westwards into rural Middlesex. After more agonising, further reflection was thought necessary and no work was carried out on the Edgware Road to Paddington scheme (except for siding tunnels west of Edgware Road station).

The Bakerloo was eventually extended to Marylebone on 27th March 1907 and Edgware Road from 15th June 1907. The station at Marylebone (one of the proposed names; the other was Lisson Grove) was actually opened under the slightly odd name 'Great Central', reflecting the name of the company serving Marylebone main line station to which it was connected by a subway running beneath Harewood Avenue; the name continued until 15th April 1917 when the present name of Marylebone was adopted. Great Central station, although superficially similar to the Leslie Green standard, was unique in being a single storey building with the ticket hall at basement level. The station building at Edgware Road was of conventional design.

The opening of Great Central to passengers did not much affect the signalling arrangements as all trains had still to use the 'down' or northbound platform. However it was decided to run test trains empty to and from Edgware Road in advance of its opening and the opportunity was taken to move the Great Central signal cabin to a more convenient location on the southbound platform at the same time, from Sunday 12th May 1907, when the southbound platform came into passenger use. Edgware Road received its own signal cabin from 12th May whereupon cabins then existed at Edgware Road, Great Central, Westminster Bridge Road, Elephant & Castle and at the depot outlet at London Road (this signal cabin was closed in 1915 and control of movements to or from the depot transferred to Westminster Bridge Road cabin). A crossover tunnel was also built at Piccadilly Circus, but only received a crossover (and signal cabin) in 1914.

Lambeth North originally opened as Kennington Road, being renamed Westminster Bridge Road after a few months. This early view shows the general arrangement, with the central arch reserved for a shop. The flat roof was designed to carry a commercial development, though this was never undertaken at this particular station. Perhaps surprisingly the company took the trouble to replace the original tiled name with new tiling. LT Museum

Great Central was unique at opening in having a surface building with the ticket hall in the basement (though Maida Vale was to follow suit). This 1914 view continues to show an inability to let out the shop units. A subway went under Lisson Grove to emerge in Marylebone main line station. The building was superseded during the Second World War and is now the site of a hotel. LT Museum

21

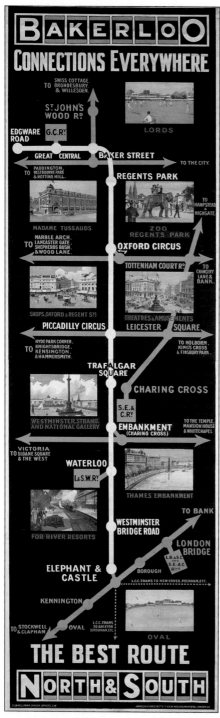

The extension to Elephant & Castle had been less troublesome and was completed and opened on 5th August 1906. On the same date Kennington Road station was renamed Westminster Bridge Road (either a pedantic technical correction or evidence of confusion with the CSLR's Kennington station). Elephant & Castle station had a substantial street level presence in the Leslie Green style, the railway being prevented from building the intended sub-surface ticket hall by clauses in its 1904 Act (put in at the insistence of the Southwark Borough Council). In addition to the main depot, stabling facilities now existed for trains in siding tunnels beyond the platforms at Elephant & Castle and, as already mentioned, Edgware Road; trains were also regularly stabled in platforms at both those stations.

The Bakerloo's compatriot railways, the Piccadilly and Hampstead, opened respectively in December 1906 and June 1907, and all three provided a broadly similar style of service. The Bakerloo interconnected with the Piccadilly at Piccadilly Circus, and shared a common station building although separate lifts were provided. Through bookings existed between Bakerloo and Piccadilly from the latter's opening and through fares between all the UERL tubes and the District Railway soon emerged. The system of through booking was soon extended to the other independent tube lines and some other railways. Physical interchange facilities already existed with the Central London Railway at Oxford Circus, the City & South London Railway at Elephant & Castle and the Metropolitan Railway at Baker Street. The first two of these had low-level interchange passages with interchange ticket offices in the subways – these closed when through bookings were introduced. In addition to through fares the three tubes soon adopted a common rule book, and company passes, staff working conditions and rolling stock all became interchangeable.

A 1908 poster used to promote the Bakerloo.
LT Museum

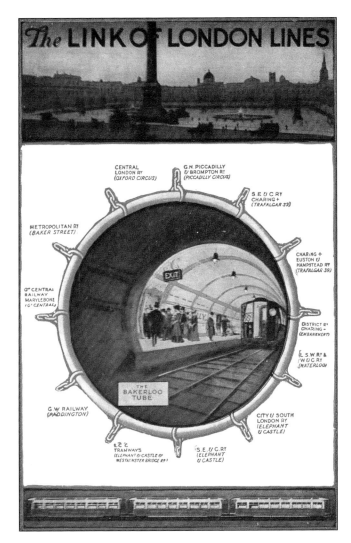

The LINK OF LONDON LINES

CENTRAL LONDON RY (OXFORD CIRCUS)

G.N. PICCADILLY & BROMPTON RY (PICCADILLY CIRCUS)

S.E.& C.RY CHARING + (TRAFALGAR SQ)

METROPOLITAN RY (BAKER STREET)

CHARING + EUSTON & HAMPSTEAD RY (TRAFALGAR SQ)

GT CENTRAL RAILWAY MARYLEBONE (G' CENTRAL)

DISTRICT RY CHARING + (EMBANKMENT)

L.S.W RY & W & C RY (WATERLOO)

THE BAKERLOO TUBE

G.W RAILWAY (PADDINGTON)

CITY & SOUTH LONDON RY (ELEPHANT & CASTLE)

TRAMWAYS (ELEPHANT & CASTLE & WESTMINSTER BRIDGE RD)

S.E.& C.RY (ELEPHANT & CASTLE)

Traffic on the Bakerloo was quite light at opening and various ideas were adopted to promote its use, including a number of postcards, of which this is one.

From 1908 agreement was reached between the UERL companies and the independent Central London, City & South London, Great Northern & City and Metropolitan Railways for the joint use of the word UNDERGROUND with large initial and final letters, often with a narrow bar above and below each of the other letters. This was applied in white on blue to station entrances to promote a common image, and at about the same time a joint map was produced for use on the respective companies' publicity. The lines – even the independent ones – had been persuaded that it was better to argue about how big they could jointly make the cake rather than haggle over the size of the slices.

The Yerkes railways were as far as possible operated as a single entity, but because each one (except the UERL itself) was a statutory company they were not free to

23

combine formally without parliament's sanction – not easily given in the face of, amongst others, a deeply suspicious London County Council. However the interdependence of the three UERL tubes was officially acknowledged in 1910 when the GNP&BR was renamed the London Electric Railway (LER) and absorbed the BS&W and CCE&H Railways. Thus the BS&WR (or Bakerloo Railway) now became the London Electric Railway's Bakerloo Line, the name it has been known by ever since. This move allowed further economies to be made and a better pooling of resources amongst the three lines. Matters were taken a stage further in 1913 when the UERL took financial control of the City & South London and Central London Railways (also tubes). These companies retained their separate legal identities, but in 1915 a new pooling scheme was adopted between all the UERL lines, which henceforth became operated as a single system. By then the London General Omnibus Company and various tramway companies were also part of the UERL fold.

A short-lived proposal for Bakerloo expansion emerged in 1908 when a junction was proposed at Edgware Road with another proposed tube line, the North West London Railway (originally authorised in 1899 to build a line from Marble Arch to Kilburn). The intention was for the Bakerloo to work the line north of Edgware Road, the Marble Arch portion being abandoned. As part of the proposal it was also intended to construct the Paddington extension, which would effectively operate as a Paddington–Edgware Road shuttle. From the Bakerloo's viewpoint the move captured the Paddington traffic whilst retaining the possibility of a future northerly extension, beyond Kilburn. However this arrangement was (perhaps fortunately) opposed and failed to obtain Parliamentary approval in the 1909 Session.

The workshops at London Road a few years after the line opened. Much of the equipment was removed when maintenance was transferred to Neasden in 1939. The shops were badly damaged during the Second World War and, although still used for stabling, lacked a roof until final demolition some forty years later. The motor car in this view has been modified since introduction with extra lamps and ventilators in the cab doors.

This view, perhaps around 1912, shows how light traffic resulted in the exit being permanently closed (people used the entrance to get out) and the shop being still unlet. Note the roller shutters used to shut off the doorways; these were replaced in the 1920s and 1930s by sliding metal gates. Visible attempts have been made to promote the 'UndergrounD' identity used by all the Underground lines in London. LT Museum

Interior of signal box at Lambeth North showing the lever frame and illuminated track diagram.

Alliance with the LNWR

1909 was a significant year for one of London's main line railways, the London & North Western (LNWR). It was in that year that it began work on a massive scheme to build two additional tracks between Watford Junction and Euston (the railway was already 4-tracks and overloaded). The new lines were to be electrified, and the intention was to divert the majority of its suburban services on to the additional lines, leaving the remainder clear for express, semi-fast and goods services.

This section of the LNWR had been a part of the historic London & Birmingham Railway whose first section, between London and Boxmoor, had opened on 20th July 1837 – the remainder of the railway north of Boxmoor opened the following year. When first opened, the only passenger station between the terminus at Euston Square and Watford (over 17 miles away) was at Harrow. Because of the steep gradients trains were at first hauled by rope and winding engine between Euston and Camden Town, a practice that continued until 1844, at about which time a station was opened there. Amalgamation with a number of other companies in 1846 transformed the London & Birmingham into the trunk portion of the London & North Western Railway, by which time a few more intermediate stations had been added. Although goods and trunk

Stairwell to Warwick Avenue station, unusually occupying some of the road space.
Commercial postcard

passenger traffic developed (requiring four tracking) the same enthusiasm was not shown towards local traffic, and by 1900 only six further stations had been added, together with a better-sited station at Watford Junction.

A little after the turn of the century the LNWR looked to developing its London local traffic. It was recognised that some of the areas through which its lines passed were not developing rapidly because of the absence of suitable stations and the limited suburban service. Inevitably the cost would be high because much of the existing route would require further (expensive) widening. The traffic potential, however, was well recognised.

The widening and the new electrified railway scheme were announced in 1906. Starting from new platforms at Watford Junction the line would take over part of the existing Rickmansworth branch (opened 1862) and turn off at a new junction just south of Watford High Street station to veer east to join and parallel the main line at Bushey. It would keep to the west side of the line as far as Wembley, where just south of the station it was to pass underneath the main line to emerge on the east side as far as Willesden Junction, where a new station would be built a little way from the existing one. South of Willesden the new line would remain on the east side to a point south of Kilburn where it would dive into large-diameter tube tunnels and run beneath the main line to serve underground stations at Loudoun Road and Chalk Farm. The line would then continue underground to Euston to serve a new platform built on an enormous reversing loop beneath the main line terminus. A number of new stations were envisaged on the new lines, in addition to which traffic from some of the existing stations would be switched to the new electric service. Powers for the scheme were obtained in 1907 but the finance was not immediately forthcoming and a start was delayed.

When work actually began on the LNWR's electric scheme in 1909 there was already some emerging uncertainty about the expensive southern end of the route and the terminal arrangements at Euston. To provide time for further cogitation the LNWR announced that work on the tube section would be left until last and that the finished sections could be worked by steam traction until everything had been completed. Work proceeded accordingly. Significantly, it was also in 1909 that the close relationship with the North London Railway was consummated with that railway being worked by the LNWR (it was taken over completely in 1922); this secured goods access to the Thames docks and passenger access to the City, at Broad Street station.

In 1911, when widening work was well advanced, the LNWR announced that the Euston loop proposal had been abandoned. A revised scheme was arrived at where instead of a single southern terminus there would now be three. City-bound passengers would get a through electric service to Broad Street (via connections at Willesden or Chalk Farm), while West End passengers would get direct trains via a new tube line from Queen's Park, joining the Bakerloo Line at Paddington. Through Bakerloo Line trains would thenceforth operate from Watford Junction to Elephant & Castle. The residue of the new service would operate to Euston via a junction with the existing tracks at Chalk Farm (LNWR), the existing main line approaches being electrified. The same announcement presaged the modernisation and electrification of the North London Railway's western group of lines to Richmond and Kew, and the LNWR/UERL route from Willesden Junction to Earl's Court. An LNWR Act of 1912 authorised the necessary junction works at Chalk Farm while an LER Act of the same year authorised an extension of the Bakerloo Line from Paddington to Queen's Park; work started in the autumn of 1912.

To Paddington and Queen's Park

The joint operation of the Watford line required the Bakerloo (still at Edgware Road) to get to Queen's Park. The LER had been quick to get powers (granted in 1911) to obtain a revised routeing between Edgware Road and Paddington, as the 1906 route was not suitable for a northerly projection. Although the modified scheme retained a good interchange with the Great Western and Metropolitan Railways, there were compromises needed to get the alignment right for extension beyond. A pragmatic, if inelegant, formula resulted in the extension swinging south after leaving Edgware Road and then embarking upon a huge, but nevertheless very sharp, curve which brought it back facing north-west.

Work began in June 1911, and, after the LER 1912 Act was passed, was expanded to include the Queen's Park extension via three new intermediate stations, at Warwick Avenue, Maida Vale and Kilburn Park (initial proposals called these stations Warrington Crescent, Elgin Avenue and Kilburn, respectively). Some financial assistance for the Queen's Park extension was made by the LNWR.

Kilburn Park station shortly before opening in 1915. LT Museum

The Bakerloo rose to the surface only just to the south of Queens Park station and this view shows the ramp which was required. A new car shed was to be erected just to the left of the ramp. LT Museum

The first section of the extension, the half-mile from Edgware Road to Paddington, opened on 1st December 1913. At last the Great Western's terminus had a convenient link with central London, a privilege for which they contributed only some £18,000. The Bakerloo's new station adopted a conventional layout at platform level, with two platforms (on a rather sharp curve) and crossover and reversing tunnels beyond; a small signal cabin was secreted in a narrow cross-passage between the platforms. But the station was novel in one respect – it was the first on the line to open from new with the access from the surface not by lifts but by means of escalators (these had been successfully employed at Earl's Court station in 1911, but only for interchange traffic); two escalators were provided astride a fixed stairway. A sub-surface ticket hall was built, with separate stairways leading up to Praed Street and the main line station, and a subway connection with an existing passage linking the main line and Metropolitan Railway stations.

The outbreak of the First World War, and other construction delays, meant the Bakerloo extension from Paddington to Queen's Park was not ready for opening until 31st January 1915. Trains ran empty between Kilburn Park and Queen's Park for a further ten days because the latter station was not quite ready (it opened on 11th February 1915) and even then the new facilities were not quite complete. Maida Vale station was also unfinished and could not be opened until 6th June 1915. At the low

Queens Park station was owned by the London & North Western Railway, although the Bakerloo had its own platforms. The station building was not untypical of the new buildings required on the Watford line to serve the new tracks, though a little larger than most. LT Museum

level the three stations were similar, with platforms flanking a lower concourse from which a pair of escalators and a fixed stairway led to the ticket hall. Platform finishes were in green (blue at Paddington) and white tiles with plasterwork ceiling. Warwick Avenue ticket hall was beneath the roadway and stairways led up to the edges of the pavement. At Maida Vale and Kilburn Park, single storey surface buildings finished in ruby-coloured glazed blocks were constructed, though at Maida Vale the ticket hall was actually in the basement.

A 1914 motor car built by Brush Engineering. These were of all-steel construction and embodied a centre door, though retaining the gated entrances as well. Similar (but not identical) cars were also built by Leeds Forge.

At Queen's Park the existing station was reconstructed by the LNWR to provide four additional platforms arranged as two islands. The LNWR local trains served the outer faces of the island platforms, though not until 1922. The inner faces were used by Bakerloo trains, which emerged from tube tunnel a quarter-mile to the south and thence ran in a steeply graded cutting to reach the level of the existing railway. A new twin-road car shed was built just to the south of the new platforms, and to the north was a further car shed, of four roads. Curiously, the outer pair of roads through the north shed actually formed part of the new route to Watford, the junction with the new LNWR lines being immediately to the north. Neither shed was quite complete at the time the extension opened.

Although the LNWR owned the station, the track and signalling was to the LER standard pattern. The signal cabin was provided with the usual miniature power frame, and the LER signals were of the semaphore type actuated by electro-pneumatic motors (coloured light signals were not used in the open-air until the 1920s). A new substation was constructed behind the passenger station at Kilburn Park, and power was supplied from Lots Road.

The extension to Queen's Park stretched the Bakerloo's allocation of rolling stock. Initially, twelve new motor cars and two new trailers were ordered in 1914 which, together with a number of spare trailers of GNP&B Railway origin, allowed several new trains to be made up. Ten of the new motor cars were built by Brush, while the other four cars were built by Leeds Forge.

Interior of one of the Brush 1914 motor cars. A spirit of transport integration may be noted, with the line diagram offering interchanges with trams and buses at certain stations, as well as other railways. LT Museum

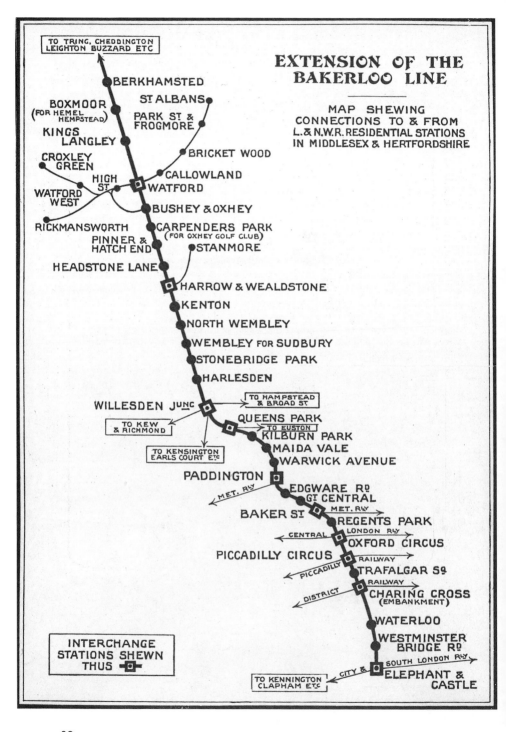

EXTENSION OF THE
BAKERLOO LINE

MAP SHEWING
CONNECTIONS TO & FROM
L. & N.W.R. RESIDENTIAL STATIONS
IN MIDDLESEX & HERTFORDSHIRE

TO TRING, CHEDDINGTON
LEIGHTON BUZZARD ETC

BERKHAMSTED
ST ALBANS
BOXMOOR
(FOR HEMEL HEMPSTEAD)
PARK ST & FROGMORE
KINGS LANGLEY
CROXLEY GREEN
BRICKET WOOD
HIGH ST
CALLOWLAND
WATFORD WEST
WATFORD
RICKMANSWORTH
BUSHEY & OXHEY
CARPENDERS PARK
(FOR OXHEY GOLF CLUB)
PINNER & HATCH END
STANMORE
HEADSTONE LANE
HARROW & WEALDSTONE
KENTON
NORTH WEMBLEY
WEMBLEY FOR SUDBURY
STONEBRIDGE PARK
HARLESDEN

TO HAMPSTEAD & BROAD ST
WILLESDEN JUNC
QUEENS PARK
TO KEW & RICHMOND
TO EUSTON
KILBURN PARK
MAIDA VALE
TO KENSINGTON EARLS COURT ETC
WARWICK AVENUE
PADDINGTON
EDGWARE RD GT CENTRAL
MET. RLY
BAKER ST
MET. RLY
REGENTS PARK
LONDON RLY
CENTRAL
OXFORD CIRCUS
PICCADILLY CIRCUS
RAILWAY
PICCADILLY
TRAFALGAR SQ
RAILWAY
DISTRICT
CHARING CROSS
(EMBANKMENT)
WATERLOO
WESTMINSTER BRIDGE RD
INTERCHANGE
STATIONS SHEWN
THUS
CITY &
SOUTH LONDON RLY
TO KENNINGTON CLAPHAM ETC
ELEPHANT & CASTLE

32

On to Watford

Some of the LNWR 'new lines' (as they were called) came into use before the Bakerloo Line reached Queen's Park. On 15th June 1912 the new lines from Harrow & Wealdstone to a point south of Willesden had come into use, together with new stations at Kenton, North Wembley, Stonebridge Park and Harlesden (and the new platforms at Willesden Junction). On the same day a new branch line to Croxley Green opened, from a junction with the existing Rickmansworth line at a point near the reconstructed Watford High Street station (this section of the branch was absorbed into the 'new' lines). The train services were initially steam-hauled, and London trains used the existing tracks to a point just north of Kensal Green tunnels, where a temporary junction and signal box were built.

Between Watford High Street and Harrow the new lines came into use on 10th February 1913, together with an additional station at Headstone Lane and a new section of track (forming the third side of a triangle) from the Croxley/Rickmansworth branches towards Bushey. A station at Carpenders Park emerged on 1st April 1914, though it closed again from January 1917 until May 1919 owing to wartime restrictions. The new lines between Kensal Green tunnels and Queen's Park were ready from 10th May 1915, on which day a 15-minute Bakerloo Line service was projected northwards from Queen's Park to Willesden Junction where the trains reversed in the bay platforms. The inauguration of this extension saw the first example of tube-sized passenger trains sharing tracks and platforms with main line trains, introducing various new operating challenges, described later. The steam service to Watford continued to operate northwards, using the outer platforms at Willesden. Power was temporarily

The LNWR had not sought to develop heavy residential traffic on its local services out of Euston, but the arrival of frequent electric trains and many new stations was to change policy significantly. Both the LNWR and Underground were to benefit considerably, and both sought to promote the new services.

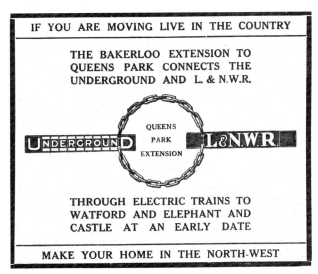

IF YOU ARE MOVING LIVE IN THE COUNTRY

THE BAKERLOO EXTENSION TO QUEENS PARK CONNECTS THE UNDERGROUND AND L. & N.W.R.

QUEENS PARK EXTENSION

UNDERGROUND   L&NWR

THROUGH ELECTRIC TRAINS TO WATFORD AND ELEPHANT AND CASTLE AT AN EARLY DATE

MAKE YOUR HOME IN THE NORTH-WEST

L.& N.W. and UNDERGROUND
RAILWAYS.

OPENING
OF THE
New Electric Line
BETWEEN
Queen's Park & Willesden

Commencing on MONDAY, MAY 10,

a QUARTER-HOURLY Service of Electric Trains on Week-days, and HALF-HOURLY on Sundays, will be run between

WILLESDEN (New Station)
AND
ELEPHANT & CASTLE

Via Queen's Park.

STATIONS—Willesden, Queen's Park, Kilburn Park, Maida Vale, Warwick Avenue, Paddington, Edgware Road, Great Central, Baker Street, Regent's Park, Oxford Circus, Piccadilly Circus, Trafalgar Square, Embankment, Waterloo, Westminster Bridge Road, Elephant and Castle.

The Timings at the principal Stations will be as under :—

	Week-days.					Sundays.		
	a.m.	a.m.	a.m.	a.m.	every 15 minutes until 12.30 night.	a.m.	a.m.	and every 30 minutes until 11.30 p.m.
WILLESDEN (New Station) dep.	5 30	5 45	6 0	6 15		8 0	8 30	
QUEEN'S PARK ... ... arr.	5 35	5 50	6 5	6 20		8 5	8 35	
PADDINGTON ... ... ,,	5 41	5 56	6 11	6 26		8 11	8 41	
PICCADILLY CIRCUS ... ,,	5 51	6 6	6 21	6 36		8 21	8 51	
ELEPHANT AND CASTLE ,,	5 59	6 14	6 29	6 44		8 29	8 59	
	a.m.	a.m.	a.m.	a.m.	every 15 minutes until 11.54 p.m.	a.m.	p.m.	and every 30 minutes until 10.55 p.m.
ELEPHANT AND CASTLE dep.	5 24	5 39	5 54	6 9		7 25	7 55	
PICCADILLY CIRCUS ... ,,	5 32	5 47	6 2	6 17		7 33	8 3	
PADDINGTON ... ... ,,	5 40	5 55	6 10	6 26		7 42	8 12	
QUEEN'S PARK ... ... ,,	5 48	6 3	6 18	6 34		7 50	8 20	
WILLESDEN (New Station) arr.	5 54	6 9	6 24	6 39		7 55	8 25	

The Trains (with a few exceptions) will call at all Intermediate Stations between Willesden and Elephant and Castle.

The 7.45, 8.0, 8.45, 9.0, and 9.45 a.m. Trains from Willesden will not call at Queen's Park, Kilburn Park, or Warwick Avenue.

The 12.39 p.m. from Elephant and Castle will run 3 minutes earlier, and the 1.9 and 1.39 p.m. Trains from Elephant and Castle one minute earlier on Saturdays.

Euston Station, May, 1915.   GUY CALTHROP, General Manager, L & N. W. Rly.

ALBERT H. STANLEY, Managing Director, Underground Rly

supplied from the Underground's Lots Road power station, as the LNWR's arrangements were not then ready. A new station at Kensal Green, initially served only by Bakerloo trains, came into use on 1st October 1916.

Although the North London Railway electrification came into use in 1916 the completion of the full LNWR scheme was severely hampered by wartime restrictions and the difficult work required at Chalk Farm. Substantial widening was required here and the junction work was exceptionally complicated; with all the flying junctions there were at one point no fewer than seventeen tracks at up to nine different levels, some climbing and some descending. However, from 16th April 1917 the new services on the Watford line were introduced to the extent that progress then allowed. Bakerloo Line trains operated a weekdays only service at about 15-minute intervals northwards to Watford Junction, and the LNWR provided a weekday, peak hours only, electric service to Watford Junction from Broad Street via Hampstead Heath; on Sundays the Bakerloo service terminated at Willesden (though from 1919 this, too, was extended to Watford). A local steam service continued to operate between Euston and Watford Junction via the new lines (cut back to Willesden on Sundays from 1919); this was augmented by additional steam trains, which plied non-stop between Euston and the new platforms at Willesden where they connected with the electric trains.

Full services were introduced from 10th July 1922 following completion of the works at Chalk Farm. From this date electric trains ran daily from Watford Junction to Euston (LNWR) and Watford Junction to Elephant & Castle (Bakerloo). Electric trains from Willesden to Broad Street via Chalk Farm (extended to Watford Junction in peak hours) supplemented these. The service to Broad Street via Hampstead Heath was withdrawn, except briefly for one trip.

The LNWR had constructed its own power station at Stonebridge Park, which came into use early in 1916 and eventually supplied power to most of its London d.c. services. Current was generated at 11,000 volts, 25 cycles per second, and was transmitted to the various substations, six of which were on the Queen's Park – Watford portion (at Bushey, Headstone Lane, Kenton, Stonebridge Park, Willesden and Queen's Park). Adjacent to the power station was the main workshop for the LNWR's new electric services and all their new stock was maintained there. In addition, a new running depot was built near Croxley Green, and this was used for stabling and minor maintenance of both LNWR and Underground stock. The LNWR also had a large minor maintenance and stabling shed at Mitre Bridge, Willesden. Signalling on the new lines was mechanically-operated, controlled generally from new signal cabins distinct from those supervising the main lines.

For the Bakerloo's Watford service it had been the intention for the LNWR and LER to purchase new stock jointly, and an order was placed with the Metropolitan Carriage, Wagon & Finance Company in 1915 for 72 new tube cars. Unfortunately the prevailing war made it quite impossible for the car builders immediately to meet this order. However, 24 new motor cars happened to be in course of delivery to the Central London Railway to service the Ealing extension, itself delayed by wartime priorities. These temporarily surplus motor cars were thus put into service on the Bakerloo Line with ex-GNP&BR gate stock trailers. Together they provided the mainstay of the Watford service for about four years, though the motor bogies on the Central London cars did not take kindly to the high speed running to Watford and had to be replaced. This stop-gap was not entirely straightforward because the platforms north of Queen's Park had been built to main line height and there was a very considerable step down into ordinary tube cars. This looming difficulty had been taxing

Top **A new train near just south of Watford High Street around the time the new lines opened. The train consists of borrowed Central London Railway motor cars and adapted trailers from the Piccadilly Line.**

Above **A 1919 view of a train on the Watford line. The Central London motor cars had to be equipped with new bogies, and to cover the work a pair of Piccadilly Line 1906 motor cars were temporarily loaned.**

the Underground Group even in 1911; the problem had even resulted in the UERL indulging in some experiments with tube stock on the South Acton – South Harrow service (then part of the Metropolitan District Railway, with full height platforms). The Board of Trade was somewhat alarmed at the makeshift arrangement of hinged and slideable steps fitted to cars in daily public service; they declined to approve the arrangement, suspecting something similar might be used on the Watford service for which powers were then being sought.

However, the use of temporary trains meant that what actually emerged on the Bakerloo's Watford trains was even more makeshift. Trains were made up of five cars, the middle three of which were of gate stock trailers. The end vestibules of these cars were fitted with a modified floor where the edges adjacent to the station platforms were raised by some 4½ inches, this being a compromise between a tube-height and a main line platform. Unfortunately the new motor cars had enclosed end vestibules where it was not possible to raise the floor because passengers would have banged their heads on the roof. North of Queen's Park passengers had therefore to negotiate as best they could what was perceived as the lesser evil of the 10-inch step between car and platform. The LER subsequently stated that they only acceded to the pressure to begin the Watford service in 1917, before they were ready, because of the LNWR's severe locomotive shortage.

The Joint Stock eventually began to arrive in 1920, in the form of 36 motor cars, 24 trailers and 12 control trailers, designed to produce twelve 6-car trains (most of the trains other than those providing the Watford service were of five cars). For the first time there was a motor car in the centre of the formation, and for this special dispensation was granted by the Board of Trade, once a number of additional safety precautions had been complied with. The car floors were a little higher than on other tube stock, which minimised the step up at the LNWR stations. Another new feature was a door in the centre of each car in addition to the usual end landings, which were now enclosed; the centre door was remotely lockable by the gatemen. The Underground Group maintained the Joint Stock, although trains did stable at Croxley Green as well. The LER owned only 24 of the cars (4 trains), the LNWR owning the rest; nevertheless the whole fleet was painted in LNWR's standard livery of chocolate with white upper panels. As a concession to main line thinking, small parcels racks were provided and, perhaps more importantly, electric heaters.

Below **Watford Joint Stock on the extension beside the London & North Western main line.**

Bottom **Interior view of one of the jointly owned trailer cars. These were the only tube-type cars to have parcel racks.** LT Museum

The Bakerloo Updated

Although the original section of the Bakerloo Line remained substantially unchanged while the thrust to the north-west was under way, there were nevertheless some significant improvements. The pre-opening reconstruction of Oxford Circus had been something of an unhappy compromise, and even by 1909 the arrangements were proving quite unsatisfactory and major changes were necessary. Powers were obtained in the LER Act 1910 for the provision of additional low-level passages, a new below-street ticket hall, and a pair of escalators connecting the two. The new ticket hall and escalators came into partial use on 9th May 1914 and when the works were complete most of the former street level ticket hall was let for commercial use.

Another troublesome station had been Embankment. The extension of the Hampstead Line from Charing Cross to Embankment in 1914 resulted in widespread changes and the excavation of a new intermediate concourse below the District Line tracks. Separate banks of escalators were installed for access to the single Hampstead Line platform and to those of the Bakerloo Line, replacing the original inclined subway. A new subway was also built to connect the Bakerloo and Hampstead Lines at low level. The District Line station entrance was rebuilt at the same time. It should be mentioned here that although these station names happen to be the same as those used for the same locations today, this period saw several potentially confusing alterations (some of which were altered back again in the 1970s). Thus from 6th April 1914 the Bakerloo Line station at Embankment was renamed 'Charing Cross (Embankment)', the Hampstead Line platforms there opening the same day and with the same name. The 'Embankment' suffix was dropped altogether from 9th May the following year, and the naming of the tube level platforms then accorded with the name of the District Railway station above. (From the same date the Hampstead's existing station at Charing Cross became 'Strand'.)

1914 was also the year when changes were made at Baker Street to improve the interchange with the Metropolitan Railway. Two escalators were introduced on 15th October 1914 to link the Bakerloo Line platforms with a new interchange concourse directly below the Metropolitan Railway's 'extension' platforms, that part of their station being rebuilt at about the same time. An interchange ticket office selling Metropolitan Railway tickets was opened in the new concourse. The Bakerloo's separate station building and lifts in upper Baker Street were retained.

Another result of the First World War was to raise fears for the security of the Bakerloo's under-river tunnels. At one point these were only three feet below the River Thames. Although nothing permanent was done during the war itself these sections of tunnel received a secondary steel protective lining during 1919/20. This subsequently proved troublesome and part of it was removed during the Second World War, with tremendous inconvenience.

Power supply arrangements at the south end of the line were enhanced from 1917 when a new substation (shared with the City & South London Railway) was opened at Elephant & Castle; this replaced London Road substation, which was taken out of use.

This control trailer, at Queen's Park, was one of some 20 cars (half control trailers, the remainder trailers) that were built by Carmmell Laird in 1920 for use on the Piccadilly Line. They were transferred to the Bakerloo in 1932, remaining in service for about six years.

The Underground continued to expand in the 1920s, and an early priority was the enlargement and modernisation of major stations in central London, in which the Bakerloo Line was to benefit. Waterloo was enlarged between 1924 and 1927 as part of the works for extending the Hampstead Line southwards from Charing Cross to Kennington. A flight of three escalators linked a new ticket hall area beneath the main line station with a low-level concourse serving both the Hampstead and Bakerloo Lines, although the existing Bakerloo lifts and ticket hall were also retained.

At Charing Cross (now Embankment) the booking hall area was significantly enlarged and a new booking office opened on 6th December 1920; new subways were also built to provide better access to the tube from street level. Additional enlargements were also made there in 1926 as part of the Hampstead Line's Kennington extension. 1926 was also a significant year at Trafalgar Square where on 13th April a pair of escalators replaced the existing lifts, though the original ticket hall was retained and modernised.

The biggest improvement was at Piccadilly Circus where the existing lifts and sloping low-level passages were replaced by escalators. A lower flight of three escalators served just the Bakerloo Line, while another flight of three served the Piccadilly Line. These six escalators converged at an intermediate level that was connected to the ticket hall level by means of a further flight of five escalators (in two shafts). The ticket hall was a vast, elliptical area built directly beneath Piccadilly Circus itself. The escalators emerged in the centre of the ticket hall, from the perimeter of which six subways and staircases brought passengers in from various street corners. One passage provided a link with the old station building which was retained to provide three further street entrances. Work began in February 1925 with the sinking of a service shaft, requiring the temporary removal of the Shaftesbury Memorial (Eros) which occupied the surface working site. Much of the construction involved the diversion of the utility service mains, for which purpose a large pipe subway had to be driven around the ticket hall site before the main excavation could begin. The new station was designed by Charles Holden & Partners, and when completed the interior finishings of the new ticket hall were luxurious and distinctly art deco in flavour. The Mayor of Westminster opened the new ticket hall, escalators and passageways on 10th December 1928, an event commemorated in one of the marble tablets.

A 3-car train at Queens Park in 1935. The leading car is a 'Feltham' motor car and the other two are Cammell-Laird trailers. Photomatic

Increasing passenger numbers quickly overwhelmed the modernised, but still cramped, facilities at Oxford Circus station. In 1923 work began once again to provide additional facilities. This time the Bakerloo's small sub-surface ticket hall was significantly enlarged; now extending below Argyll and Oxford Streets it also incorporated new escalators leading to the Central London Railway with which the ticket hall was now shared. The work was ready for opening on 5th July 1925, allowing closure of the Central London's street level building, although it did accommodate new entrance stairways. A little later a third Bakerloo Line escalator was added, in a separate shaft parallel to the existing pair, and this came into use in November 1928, following which the older Bakerloo escalators were modernised, one at a time.

The late 1920s was a period when the Underground was once more expanding, with the extension and modernisation of the Northern and Piccadilly Lines the most obvious result visible today. South-east London had not fared well in the Underground's expansion programme but considerable pressure was repeatedly brought for a south London tube to serve areas still not adequately dealt with by the Southern Railway, which had embarked on wholesale electrification of its suburban lines. One such scheme was for a Bakerloo extension to Camberwell. Such an extension, either terminating at Camberwell or continuing deep into SR territory, has been discussed or planned at various times since the early 1920s. In 1921 the Underground Group costed an extension of the Bakerloo to Camberwell, Dulwich and Sydenham. A report, dated 27th June 1922 and submitted to Frank Pick, spoke of extending the Bakerloo to Orpington via Camberwell and Loughborough Junction or Catford. Although an extension to Camberwell was endorsed by a public inquiry held by the London & Home Counties Traffic Advisory Committee in 1926, the UERL board was unconvinced and nothing was done. Operating Manager J.P. Thomas took the matter up again in 1928, suggesting an extension to Rushey Green via Camberwell and Dulwich. In 1930 an extension seemed viable, thanks to government-financed cheap capital funds for schemes to relieve unemployment, which had also assisted the much larger Piccadilly Line scheme. Parliamentary powers were obtained in 1931. The extension was to be 1¾ miles (2.8km) long, with stations at Albany Road and Camberwell, the latter beneath Denmark Hill, with overrun tunnels and sidings beyond. It was the intention to reconstruct Elephant & Castle station with escalators, a new sub-surface ticket hall and, more importantly, a third platform. The additional platform would allow a proportion of the service to be turned with remaining trains going on to Camberwell, significantly improving reversing facilities at the south end of the line and facilitating service improvements. Unfortunately the rapidly deteriorating financial position of the UERL made a start impossible; nevertheless, while the scheme was practically dead in 1932 the powers were kept alive and some detailed planning was undertaken. The extension was officially postponed in April 1937 on the grounds of cost (in particular that of steel) which had increased, in total, from £¾m to £1m per mile.

By the mid-1920s the Bakerloo Line rolling stock was becoming conspicuous for its obsolescence, both in its appearance and its technical performance. In contrast to the modernised stations about two-thirds of the Bakerloo Line's in-town service, from Queen's Park to Elephant & Castle, was still provided by antiquated and highly staff-intensive gate stock, mainly of 1906 vintage, with a few more modern cars of 1914 origin. The problem was not, of course, unique to the Bakerloo and required significant investment: a Line-by-Line programme of gate stock replacement was in due course authorised, which would allow train services to be improved. The Hampstead Line had already needed an improved style of train in 1923, to support the Edgware extension and City & South London reconstruction. For these, all-steel cars were used, based on the best of a number of sample cars made by different manufacturers. After further refinement a batch of similar cars was ordered for the Bakerloo, where the last gate stock train ran on the night of 31st December 1929. The 182 new cars were built by a UERL subsidiary, called the Union Construction & Finance Company, at premises in Feltham; consequently the cars were often referred to as Felthams. This particular order was shared with the Piccadilly Line, and to complicate matters further some cars from the Hampstead Line's 1926/7 deliveries were also transferred to the Bakerloo.

From the late 1920s 'gate stock' cars were superseded by more comfortable new cars with more door area, many built by an Underground subsidiary company at Feltham. This view shows the interior of one of the motor cars. LT Museum

Meanwhile it emerged that the Watford Joint Stock was proving slow and generally unsatisfactory; nor could it easily be adapted for air-door operation, now the standard. In consequence a further batch of 62 cars was ordered from Metropolitan Cammell in 1930 as a direct substitute. Known as the Watford Replacement Stock the cars were generally similar to the Felthams but incorporated electro-pneumatic brakes and 'weak field' motor control, features that assisted with the higher speeds operated north of Queen's Park. The new carbodies had normal Underground height floor levels, requiring the platform heights north of Queen's Park to be adjusted to a 'compromise' between main line and tube requirements. Although most of the Joint Stock cars were scrapped the London, Midland & Scottish Railway (LMS), which had inherited the lines north of Queen's Park in 1923, retained nine of its allocation of those cars. For some years they were used to operate the Croxley Green and Rickmansworth branches (the latter was electrified from 26th September 1927, but unlike Croxley Green never had through London trains); the retained cars were painted LMS crimson, though it is recorded that just one of the joint cars also operated in crimson in Bakerloo days.

The Bakerloo Line did not offer much scope for trains to do anything but call at every station, although non-stopping of certain stations was practised by Watford trains after their introduction in 1917. These missed out Regent's Park and Maida Vale all day, and Kilburn Park, Queen's Park, North Wembley, Kenton and Headstone Lane during peak hours. The range of stations not stopped at on the main line section varied over the years and defies simple description. On the section south of Queen's Park things settled down with Watford trains often only missing out Lambeth North. Non-stopping was largely abandoned after May 1938, and finally from October 1939.

One of the LMS-owned joint trains retained after withdrawal from the Bakerloo in service at Watford West on the Croxley Green branch. This branch was never served by Bakerloo trains, though they did proceed a short way to get to the so-called Croxley Green depot (which was in Oxhey). G. E. Rossiter

The 1930s rebuilding of Wembley station (Wembley Central from July 1948) was extensive and involved moving the local platforms and extending the bridge by 40 feet. All this produced space for a substantial parade of shops with the station behind, the entrances to which were comparatively modest. The ticket hall was redecorated to prevailing standards in 1988. The platforms were rafted over by an unfortunate property development in 1966, producing a feeling of unrivalled oppression only slightly mitigated by recent brightening up. LT Museum

One point of interest concerns the interworking of tube and main line trains in the event of a failure. Normally if a railway train fails completely then arrangements are made for another train to push or pull the defective train out of the way. But if some trains were tube height and some were main line height the different coupling arrangements prevented their assisting each other. In Watford Joint Stock days the ruling was that in the event of failure non-compatible trains had to be got out of the way to enable a similar train to help out. Nevertheless, a steam locomotive could help a tube train by means of a special 'match' wagon that was kept available.

When the Watford Replacement Stock was delivered a more flexible arrangement was arrived at. This stock could be fitted with what is best described as a rigid tow bar and a removable floor mounting, both of which were stowed away beneath train seats until needed. If one of these tube trains became disabled, and the following train was of main line electric stock, the equipment could be fitted in order to enable the main line train to assist the tube (the reverse was not allowed). This arrangement was continued – at least in theory – until the early 1980s.

With traffic on the new lines rising quickly the semaphore signals on the Chalk Farm to Watford section were replaced in 1932/3 by a unique coloured light system using single aspect searchlight signals and electrically operated trainstops. Signal cabins were only retained where there were points or junctions, which, together with the shunt signals, continued to be operated mechanically. At the same time the LMS and ex-LNWR trains were equipped with tripcocks, the Bakerloo trains already having them. To take advantage of the additional capacity a second reversing siding was built at Harrow to enable the service to the south to be strengthened. The overall service pattern on the Watford line did vary from year to year, but the most significant improvement was the introduction of Broad Street – Watford Junction trains on an all-day basis from 1933.

Waterloo in the 1930s. This view shows a train for Watford. Bakerloo Line stations were not then equipped with train indicators and it was felt helpful to paint a blue stripe along the side of Watford trains to help distinguish them. Even by this date the problems caused by the few curved platforms on the Bakerloo are evidenced by the various warning signs and under-platform lighting. LT Museum

These enhanced Watford services required additional 'Watford' cars, which were obtained by modifying ordinary Feltham cars re-allocated from other lines, resulting in the provision of another eight 6-car trains. The modifications included provision of e.p. brakes and weak field control, the emergency drawgear, and most importantly, heaters in the cars and driving cabs. From the late 1930s much of the older (and all new) tube stock was fitted with electro-pneumatic brakes, brake retarders and weak field control, and it was no longer necessary to have a specialised fleet for use north of Queen's Park. However, between June 1932 and 1937 trains on the Bakerloo's Watford service had a wide blue stripe painted along the carbodies, which differentiated them from the 'local' trains – destination indicators on Bakerloo Line platforms were not fitted until after the Second World War.

By July 1932, thirty-two 6-car trains were being operated on the Bakerloo Line, comprising 15 trains (and a spare) on the Watford service and 15 (and a spare) on the in-town service. This provided a 2½-minute frequency south of Queen's Park, and a roughly 7½-minute interval of Bakerloo trains between Harrow and Queen's Park with alternate trains originating from Watford Junction. The same intervals were maintained throughout the midday off-peak, though only by 3-car trains; each 3-car portion comprised one motor car, one trailer and a control trailer. Trains of six cars were the longest formation that could be used on the Bakerloo.

London Transport and the New Works Programme

After years of public debate, an entirely new type of public corporation came into existence in 1933. This was the London Passenger Transport Board (LPTB), which took control of London's bus, tramway and Underground systems from 1st July. At the same time, a standing joint committee of the LPTB and the four main line railway companies was formed; within the new Board's area the joint committee was responsible for the fares levels of all the transport concerns, together with planning policy for passenger services.

By far the largest component of the Board's acquisitions was the UERL and its transport subsidiaries, among which was the LER's Bakerloo Line. It is not surprising that the LPTB installed itself in the UERL's headquarters building – Holden's impressive block referred to as 55 Broadway. Nor is it surprising that most of the senior managers originated from the UERL, including Lord Ashfield who, many years previously as Albert Stanley, had worked on the early tube lines. There was not, therefore, any immediate change in direction in management style.

Much of the justification for the new body was the opportunity provided for substantial and co-ordinated improvements to London's public transport facilities. Within two years a massive programme of investment was launched, which became known as the 1935–40 New Works Programme. It was to have a profound effect on the future of the Bakerloo Line, though the actual changes – substantial though they were – were less dramatic than originally envisaged.

'Feltham' motor car of Watford Replacement Stock at London Road depot. For a time in the 1930s trains carried the Bakerloo Line name on the side. Differing styles were tried – see also the photo on facing page. LT Museum

45

When the initial list of New Works projects was compiled (in 1934) a £30–35 million estimate allowed for a large range of schemes, including the Camberwell extension previously dropped from the unemployment relief programme. Unfortunately rapidly increasing estimates, coupled with even greater outside pressures for extensions in north London, meant that Camberwell did not feature in the scheme put before the Treasury in 1935, though powers were kept alive and the extension featured in later plans for a possible 1940–50 New Works Programme (which allowed for possible extension beyond Camberwell over the Southern Railway to Dartford or the proposed new London airport at Lullingstone three miles south of Swanley). Two sidings and a crossover were built at Elephant & Castle along the Camberwell route using those powers; these came into use around 1940 to assist train handling at the terminus. Meanwhile the central London section of the Bakerloo Line, south from Baker Street, found a major new role thrust upon it.

The LPTB had inherited a substantial 'Underground' railway not historically part of the UERL group. This was the Metropolitan Railway whose 'extension' lines out of Baker Street served the north-west quadrant of outer London and Middlesex, and meandered into Hertfordshire and deepest Buckinghamshire. Included in this inheritance was a major bottleneck caused by these numerous branches all feeding into a main stem. South from Harrow parallel pairs of fast and slow tracks combined by means of a flat junction at Finchley Road into just two tracks through 2-mile twin tunnels to Baker Street. In this latter section were three intermediate stations, at Swiss Cottage, Marlborough Road and St John's Wood (later known as Lord's). Traffic was burgeoning as the outer suburbs developed rapidly, and the combination of just two tracks, a flat junction and local stations proved a major problem.

A scheme had been devised in 1926 where a line would be thrown off near Kilburn and drop down into a tube tunnel beneath the Edgware Road to join the Circle Line at Edgware Road station, but apart from the rebuilding of the latter nothing else was done. In a desperate attempt to ease the congestion, Marlborough Road and St John's Wood stations were closed during the rush hours from 1929. While this helped the trains to a limited extent it did nothing for local passengers who were deprived of a station at the very time they most wanted to use it, and the practice of closing the stations gradually ceased.

Another answer had to be found for this mounting problem. By the time the LPTB took over matters had been made worse by the opening of the Stanmore branch in 1932. Apart from potentially adding to the congestion, the branch diverged from the main line just north of Wembley Park station and added to the conflict at Wembley Park where, in effect, the 'fast' lines crossed the 'slow' lines on the level.

The solution adopted by the LPTB fulfilled three objectives. Firstly, it utilised some of the spare capacity of the Bakerloo Line south of Baker Street; the prevailing 24 trains per hour Bakerloo peak service could be increased to at least 32, it was considered, with fewer trains serving the Queen's Park – Paddington section. Secondly, it provided Metropolitan Line passengers with a much-desired direct access to the West End from many suburban stations, and a cross-platform service from all the others. Thirdly, it alleviated the problems of the Finchley Road – Baker Street bottleneck by effectively continuing the 4-tracking southwards.

The new tracks formed a junction with the Bakerloo Line at Baker Street, meeting up with the Metropolitan Line at Finchley Road via intermediate tube-level stations at St John's Wood and Swiss Cottage; Bakerloo trains were to be projected northwards over Metropolitan Line tracks, substituting for a proportion of the local service.

Work began in April 1936 and was pushed ahead quickly. Twin tube tunnels diverged from the Metropolitan Line station at Finchley Road, which was completely rebuilt. The tubes dived down steeply to a point near Swiss Cottage station where new tube platforms were constructed, linked by escalators to a new booking hall below the road intersection and contiguous with the Metropolitan Line station which was to remain open. Southwards below the Finchley Road the tubes continued towards a new station halfway between Marlborough Road and St John's Wood (Metropolitan), both of which were to be closed. The new tube station was situated on the corner of Wellington Road and Acacia Road and during its planning and construction was nearly always called 'Acacia Road' (though the more enigmatic 'Acacia' was toyed with briefly). Happily, it actually opened as 'St John's Wood', preserving a rather more widely understood geographical name.

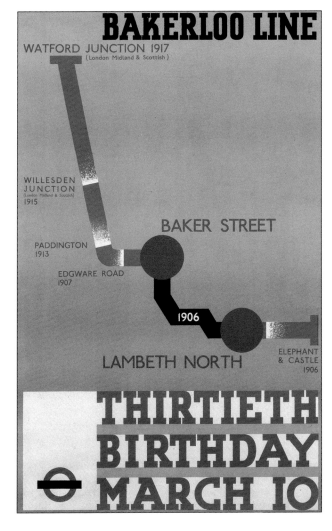

Poster by unknown artist issued in 1936 to celebrate the thirtieth anniversary of the opening of the original section of the Bakerloo Line.
LT Museum

47

At Baker Street, the new southbound line emerged into a new southbound Bakerloo platform which, together with the existing one (from Queen's Park), straddled a new concourse area from which two escalators carried passengers up to an enlargement of the existing interchange concourse under the Metropolitan Line. No additional platform was built for the northbound branch traffic, the junction being north of the existing platform. The new junction required provision of a signal cabin (opened on 29th October 1939), situated off the new lower concourse. For easier access to the Bakerloo Line a new ticket hall was also built at street level, at the corner of upper Baker Street and Marylebone Road. It was linked to an enlarged interchange concourse under the Metropolitan Line platforms, from which two pairs of escalators led to the Bakerloo. The original Bakerloo ticket hall and lifts in upper Baker Street survived until after the Second World War, though they were little used.

North of Finchley Road substantial changes were made to the existing infrastructure. Extensive track re-arrangement and signalling modernisation was undertaken with revised directions of running and some flying junctions. Most stations were altered to some extent and some were completely reconstructed. A vast modern depot was built at Neasden (on the site of the old Metropolitan Railway works), which eventually became the main maintenance facility for both the Metropolitan and the Bakerloo Lines. New signal cabins were built at Finchley Road, Willesden Green and Stanmore, with two more, one at each end of Neasden Depot.

It was not until 20th November 1939 that Bakerloo trains began operating between Stanmore and Elephant & Castle. Under the new arrangements the Stanmore branch service was entirely handed over to Bakerloo Line trains, as was most of the local service between Wembley Park and Finchley Road. South of Baker Street resignalling allowed Bakerloo Line services to be considerably intensified, to about 36 per hour in the peaks, with about half the trains originating from the Stanmore branch. (More details of the works needed may be found in The Jubilee Line book).

The original Bakerloo signals had been altered from the moving spectacle type to 2-aspect coloured light type by the mid-1920s, but the signalling layouts had not otherwise been substantially modernised except for the progressive addition of extra 'home' signals to help keep the ever-busier services on the move. An emergency crossover and signal cabin at Piccadilly Circus had also been installed in 1914, the latter being useful for evening out irregular headways. From about 1938 the automatic signalling was progressively brought up to the then prevailing standard, and the signalling south of Baker Street improved to allow for the intensified service. New signal cabins were brought into use at Lambeth North (28th January 1939), Piccadilly Circus (10th September 1939) and Elephant & Castle (2nd November 1941). The intermediate cabins at Edgware Road and Marylebone had long been removed, but new or rebuilt power-frames were provided at Paddington and Queen's Park in the existing locations. All the new power frames were of the conventional type, but at Elephant & Castle the cabin was equipped for 'route control'. Here each lever normally stood in its 'mid' position and could select one of two routes by pushing it forward or pulling it back, as the case may be; either action would set both points and signals along the selected route (and routes could to an extent be preselected). All this speeded up operation and reduced the size of the frame needed.

To increase passenger capacity, platform lengthening had become urgent. The Bakerloo had inherited platforms, each nominally 290 feet (88m) long, from pre-Yerkes days. Because each 6-car train carried two equipment compartments the train length actually available for passengers was only 5$^1/_3$ cars. On this basis the initial intention was to extend platforms to eight-car length; with traditional trains the additional intermediate motor car would increase the effective passenger space to seven cars (nearly one-third extra capacity).

However, before any work was done, the viability of a new type of train had been identified. This innovative train became known as the 1938 Stock and differed from its predecessors in having all the control equipment below the floor. By this means the whole of the car interiors were available for passenger use (except for the driving cabs). If at least some 1938 Stock were used on the Bakerloo Line, then platform extension to seven-car length was all that was necessary. It was decided to use the new style trains on the busier (Paddington) branch to mitigate the effect of the reduced train service which would inevitably result when part of the service was switched to Stanmore (in fact during the peak hour initially slightly more than half the service ran from the Queen's Park branch).

Three cars of 1938 Stock being hauled to London from the Birmingham car builders. The trucks belonged to the car builders and were used to match the tube-height couplings with those of the main line vehicles. H.C. Casserley

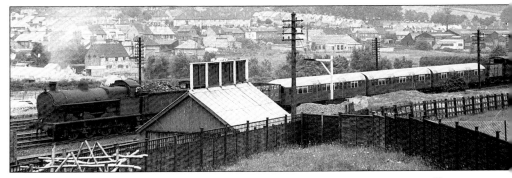

The platform extension work was complicated because it took place at the end of platforms that for most of the time were teeming with passengers, and around running tunnels that were carrying trains. Where possible only one end of any platform was extended but site conditions sometimes required short extensions at both ends. The work was severely delayed during the war and the extensions were not put into use until 1946. The whole line, including the Queen's Park and Watford services, had to put up with 6-car trains until then.

The 1938 Stock initially entered service on the Northern Line from June 1938, but from 2nd January 1939 6-car 1938 Stock trains began to enter service on the Bakerloo (spare cars, to make the trains up to seven cars, were temporarily stored). The pre-war intention was for the Bakerloo to be run by a pool of 135 cars of pre-1938 stock and 224 cars of 1938 Stock, all made up into 7-car trains. The 1938 stock was to consist of 3-car and 4-car units with automatic couplers at the outer ends, and intermediate cars semi-permanently coupled. Each outer car would necessarily be a motor car with a driving cab, and each unit would also contain a trailer; the 4-car unit would also contain a motor car, but without a cab. Of the 64 trailers 52 (later 58) would actually be cars of 1927 vintage, modified to run with the new cars. The old stock would operate in 7-car formations on the Stanmore service while the newer, higher capacity trains would operate on the busier Queen's Park and Watford service. By January 1940 some 28 of the line's 45 trains were of 1938 Stock, including the entire Queen's Park–Watford service of 25 trains.

Interior of a 1938 Stock non-driving motor car. LT Museum

A blast wall at one of the entrances to Piccadilly Circus station. LT Museum

However, in these troubled times events caused the plan to be changed irreversibly. A substantial mileage of the Northern Line's extensions had been curtailed during the war and many 1938 Stock cars were therefore temporarily surplus to requirements. Meanwhile the new cars on the Bakerloo had not run well with the old stock because of their different operating characteristics – the new trains kept catching up the older ones, giving rise to uneven headways. With all this in mind the decision was made to put as much as possible of the spare 1938 Stock into Bakerloo service in preference to old stock which was stored instead. As the new trains were of higher capacity and the platform lengthening work had been delayed by the war, this move made sense for other reasons too. By 1946 there were only five old stock trains still running on the Bakerloo. Following completion of platform lengthening in the same year the stored 1938 Stock cars were introduced into the new trains lengthening them to seven cars.

The war inevitably impacted on the services the Underground provided. This was partly because of the various civil defence measures which needed to be taken for safety and security reasons, partly because of the air raids and bomb damage itself, and not least because of the adoption of Underground stations by local residents as public shelters. Attempts to discourage sheltering failed lamentably, even though they were by no means necessarily safe places. Thus tube station platforms were soon equipped with bunks, toilets, first aid posts and all the other paraphernalia needed to look after the thousands of people who teemed in at night; special tickets were even issued to try and maintain some sort of control.

The obvious signs of wartime defence included the erection of blast walls outside many station entrances and the removal of some signs, where thought visible from aircraft. Reduced lighting near entrances and at open-air stations was another feature – resulting in the use of much white paint to make things stand out to passengers. Netting, to reduce possible splintering near bomb blast, covered train windows, and reduced lighting was installed for use while trains were in the open-air.

South end of
southbound platform
at Lambeth North
after the raid on 16th
January 1941; 20
people were injured.
The tunnel crown is
only about 48 feet
beneath street level.
LT Museum

The under-river tunnels created worry in the event of a large bomb landing nearby. As a precaution it was decided to equip Charing Cross and Waterloo stations with steel floodgates, which could be slid across the tunnel entrances to seal the under-river sections during air raids. The gates, which could be manoeuvred both electrically and by hand, were interlocked with the signalling to avoid a train becoming trapped between the gates (or running into a closed gate). The gates were just ready for the breakout of war but hadn't even been started during 1938 when the Munich crisis was at its height. With war believed imminent it was decided to close and seal the under-river tunnels from 20.00 on 27th September, resulting in the closure of the Bakerloo south of Piccadilly Circus. Temporary peace allowed the concrete plugs to be demolished in time for services to resume on 8th October 1938. This did serve to demonstrate that the single crossover at Piccadilly Circus was not sufficient to reverse the service if the floodgates were often closed, and the trailing crossover layout was converted to 'scissors' during 1939 (it was also done at Lambeth North). Floodgates were supplemented by hand operated flood doors at many stations and in interchange passageways, primarily to address threats from broken sewers and water mains.

The Bakerloo received its share of bomb and (later) rocket damage. Stations hit included Marylebone, Swiss Cottage, Finchley Road, West Hampstead, Trafalgar Square, Stanmore and Oxford Circus, though several others sustained minor damage from blast nearby. In most cases damage was repairable. At Lambeth North the southern end of the platforms were very badly damaged by a raid in January 1941, when a bomb exploded directly above; the service was suspended south of Waterloo for three months, until the platforms had been made safe enough for use. London Road depot was hit, more than once, with some rolling stock being damaged as well as the depot structures. Tracks were frequently hit, creating temporary disruption. Between Swiss Cottage and St John's Wood a bomb above even caused cracks to tunnel segments. More seriously, at Kilburn in September 1940 a 70-feet section of the northbound viaduct was demolished by a high explosive bomb, causing havoc to Metropolitan and Bakerloo trains for some time. Makeshift repairs were done with wooden propping, but proper repairs took months.

Modernisation – but not Expansion

After the war it became evident that the remaining Northern Line extensions would never be completed – the 1938 Stock 'temporarily' running on the Bakerloo could remain there. This decision was not without its problems. While the bulk of the 1938 Stock was intended to run in 7-car formations, some trains on the Northern Line had originally been intended to run in 6-car and 9-car formations, and the mix of cars had been ordered accordingly. However the imperative to press as many new (7-car) trains into service had long since exhausted the pool of correct cars and was now resulting in an increasing number of strange and inflexible formations. As a palliative there was a further revision to the overall 1938 Stock allocation, producing more 7-car trains mainly of non-standard formations. Most of these changes had taken place by 1949. In spite of increasingly frenetic attempts to press the remaining new cars into service there would inevitably be a final rump of some 41 modern cars that were virtually unusable in their existing form.

The outcome was a comprehensive revision to tube stock allocation involving new cars and extensive conversion work. The 91 new cars (the 1949 stock) were ordered from the Birmingham Railway Carriage & Wagon Company. The conversion work standardised formations and non-standard cars, and absorbed a number of experimental cars which were in store. Apart from standardisation (and the mopping up of unused new cars) all this allowed a significant number of additional trains to be generated.

1938 Stock train at Dollis Hill around 1947 on the branch of the Bakerloo that is now part of the Jubilee Line. J. Voerman

The 1949 cars were of two types – 21 were trailers and 70 were motor cars incorporating an automatic coupler at one end and a simplified driving control cabinet locked behind an end panel in the passenger saloon. These driving controls were designed for use purely during shunting, being a much cheaper option than the provision of a full driving cab; of course, this restricted use to the middle of full length trains. The new cars were eventually distributed amongst the 1938 Stock fleet on the Northern, Bakerloo and Piccadilly Lines, and the remarshalling task was completed during 1953. The Bakerloo's allocation was now 54 trains, over half of which incorporated the 1949 cars with shunting controls only.

'NEW VIEW' COACH FOR THE BAKERLOO NEXT WEEK

An experimental "vista" car which will be in use on the Bakerloo Line next week.

Principal feature is the series of glass panes from floor to roof.

Hitherto standing passengers have had to crane their necks to see out. Now they will have a direct eye-level view out of the car.

Further innovation: large porthole-shaped windows to admit light through recesses into which sliding-doors open.

The experimental car has been adapted from a normal vehicle.

As a prelude to the intended introduction of new rolling stock on the Piccadilly and Central lines, an accident-damaged Bakerloo Line car was heavily modified to demonstrate some new ideas. The main difference was the extension of window glazing into the roof so that standing passengers could see out. The car ran in this form on the Bakerloo from 1949 until 1952 and then went to the Northern Line.

Following the reconstruction of Piccadilly Circus in 1928 the Bakerloo had to wait some time for further station improvements. A 1937 scheme planned to replace the existing three lifts at Marylebone with a pair of escalators leading directly up to the main line station concourse, where much of the traffic interchanged. This meant a new subway leading from the existing lower lift landing and beneath Harewood Avenue, thence a particularly long escalator shaft. Significantly this was not part of the New Works Programme, and was funded entirely by LT who were finding the existing station arrangements increasingly inconvenient. Work could not well be abandoned in

Approach to Piccadilly Circus from the north. The need to extend platforms in the 1930s brought the northbound platform into the crossover itself, requiring some intricate works to enlarge the crossover tunnel. The fluorescent lighting was installed in 1946.
LT Museum

The entrance to Marylebone Underground station in the 1950s. LT Museum

wartime conditions as the shaft was partly completed and lay in water-bearing ground. Matters were pursued on a temporary basis (encouraged by the bombing of the old station) and the escalators and temporary ticket office on the main line concourse opened on 1st February 1943. The 'temporary' surface structure, of pre-cast blocks, scaffolding and corrugated iron, survived until a new ticket office, selling both Underground and main line railway tickets, opened in December 1988.

After the war the government embarked on a massive programme of nationalisation. The 1947 Transport Act led on 1st January 1948 to most of Britain's inland surface transport systems passing into the control of the British Transport Commission (BTC). The Underground (with the rest of the LPTB) became part of the BTC, though the day-to-day control of the former LPTB operations was delegated to a subsidiary body, the London Transport Executive (LTE). Perversely, this courageous attempt at transport integration never produced in London anything like the benefits generated by the financial imperatives of the 1933 pooling of revenues between London Transport and the main line railways.

By 1948 the level of service scheduled on the trunk section of line south of Baker Street had increased to 36 trains per hour, the maximum service level practicable – though still not enough. One of the main factors that made it difficult to improve service frequencies further was the simple, two-platform layout at Elephant & Castle. As it was, the turnaround time for trains here was about two minutes. This was insufficient

The space (unwanted by passengers) at Lambeth North was exploited by the Underground's central staff training school from 1920, soon to be joined by the clothing store and the recruitment section. The unwanted shop unit was adapted as the entrance to the basement and upper storeys. The substation next door feeds the Northern Line which runs nearby. LT Museum

From 1948 the building was rearranged, with the entrance being moved into the disused exit, and a new ticket office being built. The original entrance was incorporated into the new offices (and the shop unit, at last, let). The training centre was removed to White City in 1963 whence the premises were occupied by the ticket inspectorate. LT Museum

to allow incoming traincrews to walk back along the platform and required a process called 'stepping back', where there were more crews than trains and the incoming crew took a later train away. By this time Elephant & Castle was the only one of the original 'Yerkes' tube termini remaining, and its 2-platform layout was totally unsuitable for prevailing operations. So the time was right to consider either an improved terminal arrangement with three platforms, or to examine once more the proposed Camberwell extension for which the powers still survived and which were once more renewed in 1948.

After much local agitation Lord Latham, the Chairman of LT from 1948, announced that a 1½-mile (2.1km) extension would be undertaken. The improved reversing facilities at Camberwell would allow an increase in service levels throughout the line (to 40 trains per hour), with LT consequently needing to purchase an additional 14 trains; in turn this would need a new depot, to be built at Stanmore, costing £600,000 and requiring parliamentary powers. The depot envisaged seven double length sidings outdoor, with a 6-road car shed (incorporating a 2-road lifting shop). The whole scheme was estimated to cost about £4.5m. It was anticipated that work would begin in January 1950 with the sinking of five working shafts. Tunnelling would start in February or March, and was expected to take place entirely in compressed air because of the water-bearing ground; this was believed likely to be the biggest tunnelling job ever in compressed air in London and involve over 500 men, with 150,000 tons of earth to be disposed of. The whole scheme was expected to take about three years to complete. With BTC authorisation already given, the extension began to appear as 'under construction' on the Underground Map and some station signs.

The station at Camberwell was intended to be beneath the 'Green' itself, on a quite different site to that envisaged in 1931. Under this scheme Elephant & Castle would retain its 2-platform layout, but without regular reversing: three platforms were to be built at Camberwell Green instead. An intermediate station was now planned at Walworth Road, rather than Albany Road, which was a little further south. Preliminary works and test borings were undertaken, mainly during 1949.

Though the improved terminal arrangements were viewed as important, all the 'extras' that had appeared quickly began to sow doubts. Furthermore, engineering difficulties (focusing around ground conditions) had now emerged, and the more detailed evaluations prior to the tendering process showed that the project would cost £6¼m and could not possibly be afforded in the prevailing financial climate; money was not forthcoming from the government, and the financial position of the BTC was steadily worsening. Perhaps more relevantly, the huge post-war traffic increases on the Underground had levelled off and, if anything, had begun to decline. The immediate pressure for improving terminal facilities for traffic purposes had abated – there was little other crucial need for the extension, though local pressure was maintained for some time. Work did not begin as planned in January 1950 and it was obvious the scheme was in deep trouble. The result of the tenders was presented to the BTC in July 1950; with no sign of encouragement they felt moved to make any decision the Minister's problem and he was not minded to be supportive either. It was not, however, until 29th September 1950 that LT publicly regretted the necessity to 'defer' the extension. Notwithstanding a proposition made as recently as 1946 that the Bakerloo might be extended even beyond Camberwell, to Herne Hill, the climate now couldn't have been more different. The twin tunnels and crossover south of Elephant & Castle, completed in 1940 under powers for the Camberwell extension and utilised as sidings, remain the only physical evidence of the planned southerly projection.

Facing page
Some work for the Camberwell extension took place on site, including the digging of boreholes to test ground conditions. Popperfoto

Left **Camberwell** was a sufficiently certain proposition to appear on some station signs of the period, such as this one at Kilburn Park, where attempts to paint it out have not been entirely successful. R. Collen-Jones

BAKERLOO LINE
CENTRAL LINE
CIRCLE LINE
DISTRICT LINE
METROPOLITAN LINE
NORTHERN LINE
PICCADILLY LINE

FURTHER ELECTRIC SERVICES PROPOSED

STATION   INTERCHANGE STATION

Although the powers renewed in 1948 included an intermediate station, it is uncertain that this would have been built, at least initially. When the planned extension appeared on the 1949–50 Underground maps no station other than Camberwell itself was shown. Ideas of an extension to Camberwell date back to 1921 (see page 40). LT Museum

Pre-war normality resumed on the Bakerloo Line from June 1950 when full-length trains again ceased to run during the slack periods; 3-car portions of trains were stabled, leaving 4-car trains in service. This gave rise to some difficulties at Watford where the 3-car portion had to be driven 1½ miles (2.1km) via Watford High Street to Croxley Green depot. The arrival of 1949 stock meant that on many trains the stabling portion had to be driven on passenger lines from the 'shunting' control panel within the passenger saloon. This quickly proved unpopular with crews and caused stock to be re-allocated with the Piccadilly Line so that fifteen normal 3-car units were always available for use on the trains due to uncouple at Watford.

From December 1949 passenger door control had been introduced on the open sections of the Bakerloo Line; this was a pre-war idea that had not been entirely satisfactory, and the equipment was much modified as a result of the earlier experiences. The idea was that out of the rush hours passengers could open the doors adjacent to them from push buttons next to those doors (under the overriding control of the guard); this cut down wear and tear on doors through which no-one wished to board, and in cold weather helped to keep the cars warm. Neither passenger door control nor uncoupling proved sufficiently advantageous to outweigh the operational and maintenance complications which then resulted. They were abandoned respectively in 1959 and 1961.

A 1938 Stock driving motor car sweeps into Swiss Cottage station in 1951. Some trains received destination plates showing the southern terminus in full, although on this stock most were abbreviated to 'Elephant'.
LT Museum

60

A 3-car 1938 Stock unit at Queens Park (Uncoupling non-driving motor leading). It is proceeding from the north shed to the south shed for stabling during the off-peak period when only 4-car trains were run. After the last war, uncoupling took place at Queens Park (usually in the north shed), Watford Junction and Stanmore.

Two 1938 Stock units stabled off-peak at Watford Junction around 1950. This electrified bay (no longer there) was alongside the original station rather than the new platforms used for the electric services.

At Waterloo the Festival of Britain activities on the South Bank brought heavy additional traffic to the Waterloo area and in anticipation of this a bank of three escalators was built from the lower tube station level to a new ticket hall near the exhibition site; these opened in May 1951. A few years later the construction of the Shell Building near the top of this shaft gave the opportunity for LT to construct a new permanent ticket hall at street level beneath the new building, and two of the three 'exhibition' escalators were utilised (the centre escalator was removed for use at Green Park and a staircase substituted). The entrance was closed for reconstruction in 1957 and the new ticket hall opened in 1962 (it was closed again during 1999 for major refurbishment and re-opened in November of the same year). Charing Cross station also received attention during the Festival of Britain works, and two new escalators were provided to link the ticket hall level with the interchange concourse to the Bakerloo and Northern Line platforms.

By the 1950s the conditions at Oxford Circus station had once more deteriorated badly. Despite alterations to the passageways to the Bakerloo Line, the layout at low level was still quite inadequate. To try and ease matters a pair of high-speed lifts was installed in 1942 to supplement the escalator service, but conditions remained most unsatisfactory and brief periods of closure in the evening peak to relieve crowding were commonplace. Reconstruction had been contemplated for many years but nothing was done because of a combination of very difficult site conditions and the emerging Victoria Line scheme, whose routeing via Oxford Circus would of itself generate a need for major reconstruction.

Although powers for the Victoria Line were granted in 1955, government authority (an essential prerequisite to the funding) only arrived in August 1962. Within a few weeks work began on the enormous task of reconstructing Oxford Circus station, judged to be one of the longest tasks of the overall project. What emerged was a vast new circular ticket hall underneath the 'circus' itself, with entrances in each quadrant to both sides of each street. From this ticket hall four escalators led to an intermediate level from where two pairs of escalators led to Bakerloo Line level (one pair to each platform). These latter escalators would also serve the Victoria Line when it opened, and were largely used to carry 'Way In' traffic. The existing three Bakerloo Line escalators and the old ticket hall were retained and used exclusively to carry 'Way Out' traffic. Most of the old low-level subways were swept away and replaced with new passages mainly carrying one-way flows. New interchange passages to the Central Line were built. The new ticket hall was opened in 1968, and this section of the Victoria Line opened on 7th March 1969.

During 1957/58, while the go-ahead for the Victoria Line had still been awaited, planners had taken a further look at the possible options for future tube extensions south of the River, a need still being perceived. For practical purposes the options were either a continuation of the Victoria Line south from Victoria, or of the Bakerloo Line beyond Elephant & Castle. In the latter case it was felt that a natural route for the Bakerloo would be towards what was then north Kent, but this would attract more traffic than the overcrowded central section of the Bakerloo Line could cope with and a more modest extension was all that was felt prudent.

Brixton was considered a reasonable objective, either for the Victoria Line or for the Bakerloo Line via Camberwell (for which there was still some moral commitment). In the end it was clear that the most justifiable extension on traffic, revenue and cost grounds was that of the Victoria Line, which reached Brixton in 1971. Parliamentary powers for Camberwell itself were allowed to lapse in 1961.

An early 1970s map of the planned extension to Peckham.

POSSIBLE BAKERLOO LINE
EXTENSION TO PECKHAM

Perversely, it was not long after abandoning those parliamentary powers that new circumstances made a southwards Bakerloo extension a serious proposition again. At the end of 1962 the BTC was abolished and London Transport and British Railways passed to separate new boards directly responsible to the Minister of Transport. Co-ordination, of a sort, was maintained through various joint committees. In 1964 the joint LT and BR 'Passenger Transport Planning Committee for London' desired that a Camberwell route continue to be studied "but not as a task of first priority". By now a further limited extension beyond Camberwell to Peckham Rye was being considered; the thinking behind this was that part of the justification for such an extension would be the rationalisation and relief of overcrowding on sections of BR's Southern Region services. Later studies confirmed the desirability of such an extension and reiterated the unsatisfactory nature of the terminal at Elephant & Castle. The feeling was that the justification for an extension to Peckham was such as to make the route worth physically safeguarding.

The case for a southern extension became stronger in the late 1960s. First, there was an LT Fleet Line project, described in the next chapter, to relieve the central London sections of the Bakerloo of its worst overcrowding, which would in turn create more capacity for an extension beyond Camberwell. Secondly, there was the 1963 London Government Act which two years later created the various London Boroughs and the Greater London Council. Local boroughs were given stronger and louder voices to argue their case, and Southwark pressed LT hard for an extension into the borough. As a result, in 1969, a joint working party between Southwark and LT was established to develop the Peckham proposal further. The transfer of London Transport on 1st January 1970 from central to local political control in the form of the GLC was another factor favouring examination of this type of extension. Finally, government grants were available following the 1968 Transport Act; these potentially covered up to 75 per cent of capital costs of such schemes (but actually getting the money was not necessarily going to be an easy task).

A Peckham extension was thus viewed by all interested parties as a nice-to-have railway – providing central government were willing to pay for it. As quickly as November 1970 it was viewed as one of the next logical developments after the Fleet Line and the Piccadilly Line extension to Heathrow. By 1972 Peckham was being included in the GLC's ambitious 20-year plans, and in LT's 10-year capital estimates.

A platform view of Waterloo in the early 1960s. Fluorescent lights, modern signs and innumerable advertisements serve to disguise (and then only partially) the 1906 infrastructure. Under-edge lighting (originally lit only when a train was in the platform) dates back to the 1920s and helped draw attention to the large gap between doors and platform edge which arises on a curved platform. The 'suicide' pit between the tracks dates from the mid-1930s. LT Museum

A 1973 view at Finchley Road of one of the 1927-built trailers still serving as part of the 1938 Stock fleet. A.J. Robertson

By 1974 detailed planning had been undertaken and precise estimates made. However, while the extension would undoubtedly have improved transport facilities in the area, the cost-benefit analysis was unconvincing. Even with capital costs paid the line would not produce a very worthwhile return because so much traffic would be siphoned off existing services. In other words the money would probably be better spent on something else.

In the absence of any compelling reason to proceed with the line urgently it was agreed to refer the scheme to the London Rail Study, and the intended parliamentary powers were not sought for the time being. The Rail Study reported in November 1974 and did not favour the extension to Peckham, labelling it as a "weak case" in planning as well as transport terms. It became increasingly clear that it would not be a high priority for the vital 75 per cent grant from government, who were procrastinating even about tube railway schemes that had much higher GLC priority.

A further nail in the Peckham coffin was London Transport's proposal for an extensive network of 'Speedbuses' along key roads to be favoured with exclusive bus lanes – one such route was intended to serve Peckham. The Speedbus in theory produced most of the social benefit of a new railway at a fraction of the costs. Bakerloo extension southwards was therefore forgotten and route safeguarding was abandoned. In the event, Speedbus did not happen either. Elephant & Castle remains as a terminus an increasing anachronism, tolerated only because service levels have been able to be reduced as part of the Fleet Line scheme, described next; but in planning terms it is much too close to modern central London.

From Fleet Line to Jubilee Line

After the 55-year gap between the opening of the Hampstead Tube in 1907 and authorisation of the next central London tube, the Victoria Line, in 1962, LT were now quick to follow on with a further central London railway; intended to run east-west beneath Fleet Street and thence towards south-east London. This came to be called the Fleet Line. Its ancestry goes back to a number of pre-Second World War and wartime railway schemes, but a more immediate cause was the problem of the inadequate services which were all that could be provided on the northern branches of the Bakerloo Line so long as they both converged on Baker Street.

The 1939 Stanmore service had in some respects transferred the Metropolitan Line's problems to the tube services below. It was not reliably possible to offer much more than a 4-minute interval service on either branch, and traffic levels demanded better, particularly to Paddington. Similarly, the section of Bakerloo Line south of Baker Street was heavily overcrowded and some sort of relief was required. This need became acute once cross-platform interchange existed with the Victoria Line at Oxford Circus.

Numerous options were considered, including the takeover of the Queen's Park branch by a new line, or a new direct tube line from Paddington to the West End instead of the more circuitous route via Baker Street. In the event, the Fleet Line project addressed these problems by duplicating the Bakerloo Line between Baker Street and Trafalgar Square (but via Bond Street and Green Park) and by taking over the Stanmore branch. The Bakerloo would thus revert to its pre-1939 state with the main service running from Elephant & Castle to Queen's Park with some trains projected to Watford. LT's new masters at the GLC were anxious to proceed with the Fleet Line, themselves meeting 25 per cent of the capital cost of a first stage. This would produce a 'new' railway from Stanmore, via Baker Street, to its own terminal platforms at Charing Cross station, providing low-level interchange with the Bakerloo Line (at Trafalgar Square) and the Northern Line (at Strand) – as well as interchange with main line trains.

The go-ahead was given in August 1971, with 75 per cent government financial support, and tunnelling began in February 1972. During the year of the Queen's Silver Jubilee in 1977 the GLC decided to rename the new line the Jubilee Line, which name it has had ever since. The Jubilee Line opened after considerable delay on 1st May 1979. On the same date the Bakerloo Line service reverted to its Watford Junction to Elephant & Castle routeing. As a part of all this some existing station names in the Charing Cross area – which had never really been satisfactory – required changing. Thus Trafalgar Square (now part of an enlarged station serving the Jubilee Line and the Northern Line at Strand) became Charing Cross (on 1st May 1979), while the former Charing Cross station became Embankment (from 12th September 1976), after an interim familiarisation period of Charing Cross Embankment (from 4th August 1974). This, of course, restored the name it had had at opening.

The platform finishings at Baker Street were still of BS&WR origin, and were

Sherlock Holmes in the tiling at Baker Street. Capital Transport

severely affected by the considerable Jubilee Line construction works and additional passageways which were driven; nor were they going to be easily harmonised with the brand new finishings in the new platforms and corridors. Major renovation was the only answer, and then only when the Jubilee Line activities were complete. This involved complete re-tiling of the Bakerloo Line platforms, escalator shafts, access passages and the intermediate concourse under the Metropolitan Line platforms. Following the Jubilee Line theme, the new tiling was based on a repeating caricature of Sherlock Holmes's head, complete with pipe and deerstalker. The work was completed in 1982.

The loss of the Stanmore branch meant loss of ready access to the Bakerloo's maintenance depot at Neasden: an alternative would be required. London Road depot had long since ceased to be a major maintenance facility, and was now merely a number of stabling sidings among ruined buildings (the car shed had lost its roof in the war, but the walls remained). Initially it was hoped that the extension to Peckham would offer opportunities for a major new depot, and a site between Peckham Rye and Nunhead was notionally set aside. The proposed site was on the south side of the line near

Nunhead with provision for 15 roads. It was an expensive site in that much property demolition and road alteration would have been needed. When it became evident that the Peckham extension would not proceed a new depot site was urgently sought along the Elephant & Castle – Watford axis, preferably close to the tube tunnel section where the train service was densest.

The site eventually chosen was adjacent to the British Railways section just north of Stonebridge Park station on the 'new' lines (now generally called the d.c. lines to distinguish them from the a.c. overhead services). Local residents were not pleased at the prospect of living next to a new depot (which superseded the delights of the power station and some carriage sidings) and won several concessions at a planning inquiry on environmental grounds; all this caused some worrying delay. Preparatory re-signalling of the BR line in the Stonebridge Park area was commissioned in January 1977; the new depot itself was commissioned on 8th January 1979 and came into use from 9th April. The depot comprised a two-road lifting shop with six maintenance roads alongside, and seven other stabling sidings (six under cover). All train movements were controlled from an elevated central control tower, and within the depot site was an LT substation so the tracks could be quite independent from the British Rail power supply. A small number of additional sidings were added later as train services were improved.

The depot location at Stonebridge Park also served to maintain the Bakerloo Line's tie to the main line suburban tracks north of Queen's Park. Here was an outlet which had seen little change in Underground service frequencies between the introduction of Sunday tube trains in 1919 and the mid-1960s, but which had seen a drastic cut-back in through tube trains by the early 1970s. The latter history of this section of the Bakerloo Line is now looked at in more detail.

Stonebridge Park depot in course of construction. Ian Robins

Watford Run-Down

There had been few station alterations north of Queen's Park since 1919. A new station opened at South Kenton on 3rd July 1933 and Stonebridge Park (burnt down in 1917) was burnt down again in 1945 and rebuilt at platform level in 1948. Carpenders Park was relocated in 1952 (just south of the former station), though new buildings were not formally opened until 1954. New station buildings were also erected at Wembley Central and incorporated a shopping arcade; the work was started before the war, but completion was protracted.

The power supply arrangements north of Queen's Park carried on without much change until the 1940s when Stonebridge Park power station was updated and converted to 50-cycle operation with a capacity of 38 megawatts. New substation equipment was installed, largely at new sites (between Watford and Queen's Park the locations were: Watford, Bushey, Hatch End, Harrow, Kenton, Wembley, Harlesden, Willesden and Queen's Park). The power station continued to operate until 30th July 1967 when current was obtained from the National Grid instead. The building survived a few years longer but was demolished prior to part of the site being used for the new Bakerloo Line depot.

The original Oerlikon stock used by British Railways on the Watford line had reached the end of its useful life by the mid-1950s and was replaced by new slam-door

A 1982 view of a 1938 Stock train arriving at Queens Park. R.G. Bradford

trains between 1957 and 1959 (one of the old Oerlikon cars is preserved in the National Railway Museum). The new stock was of unrevolutionary, even obsolescent, design arranged in 3-car sets of mixed saloon and compartment formation, with one car on each set motored. In peak hours trains initially worked in 6-car formations. The BTH/GEC cars of 1928–32 vintage remained in service for a few more years, until service reductions meant they, too, could be scrapped.

Unremarkable as the Watford line had been to British Railways and its predecessors, the long haul out to Watford was never regarded as a great success either by the Underground. Even prior to LPTB days it was thought to be impacting badly on the reliability of the Bakerloo Line as a whole. It was discovered problematic to mix a short in-town service whose performance depended on even train intervals with less frequent long-haul services where timekeeping was the keynote. Furthermore, any problems on the LNWR electric services soon transmitted their effects to the Bakerloo. The relatively high-speed running was also thought to be having an adverse effect on rolling stock and was inviting questions about passenger comfort on tube stock, which wasn't really suitable for long distances.

Nevertheless the Bakerloo service remained at a fairly constant level until well after the Second World War; essentially there was a 7½-minute peak interval between Queen's Park and Harrow, and 15-minutes northwards. During the midday off-peak period a basic 20-minute Bakerloo service operated to Watford Junction, with a Broad Street and a Euston service in between each of the Bakerloo trains. From the early 1960s the local line services were progressively reduced as traffic levels dropped. One of the first casualties was the off-peak BR service from Watford to Broad Street, which ceased in August 1962.

The reason for the previous stability of the tube service was not hard to see. The track and the stations north of Queen's Park were owned by British Railways, and it was that organisation which dictated service levels; LT was paid to operate an appropriate number of trains. Of course, when BR became more desperate to reduce costs the LT services were next in line for scrutiny. It was the through off-peak Bakerloo Line service which was the next casualty of BR retrenchment. From the June 1965 timetable Bakerloo Line trains operated north of Queen's Park only in the rush hours, and through off-peak passengers had to change for the West End. Six Bakerloo trains ran south from Watford in the morning, and towards Watford in the evening, and an additional four trains ran to and from Harrow in both peaks. The Watford trains all started from or were stabled at Croxley Green shed. The BR services were also reduced further at the same time.

The May 1966 timetable saw the through Watford trains reduced to four, one-way in each peak. The February 1970 timetable saw the four Harrow trains withdrawn (partly because of the increasing unreliability of 1938 Stock), leaving the Bakerloo Line with just four through Watford Junction trains in the rush hours, southbound in the morning and northbound in the evening. By this time the BR Watford service consisted of a 15-minute interval service between Watford Junction and Euston, all day, with extra rush-hour trains to Broad Street about every 15 minutes. The maximum peak-hour service through Willesden Junction was now only 13 trains.

Also in 1970 the British Railways d.c. trains were converted from a 4-rail, insulated return, traction system to the 3-rail system widely used elsewhere on BR. To allow the Bakerloo Line trains to continue to operate north of Queen's Park the centre (fourth) rail was retained, but was bonded to one of the running rails and earthed (the negative rail was also retained south of Queen's Park to Kilburn High Road where there was an emergency crossover). Used by so few trains a day, the centre rail became a further source of unreliability. In addition, the new arrangements did put heavy demands on the deteriorating insulation of the 1938 Stock's electrical system, and this became a further source of unreliability.

The 4-train Bakerloo service to Watford Junction was maintained for another decade, the operational convenience of the Croxley Green Depot just outweighing the service unreliability complications (it was considered the Bakerloo could not stand the capacity reduction of four trains, but no more convenient siding accommodation was available). The fact that payment was received was also a factor in the Watford outpost being served for so long. However, when Stonebridge Park depot opened in 1979, LT had to pay BR for the additional LT trains running between Queen's Park and Stonebridge Park depot, BR regarding these as surplus to the basic Watford line timetable which itself had been reduced further during the mid-1970s.

In 1982 the political and legal climate following the House of Lords judicial decision on LT subsidy caused widespread service reductions to meet more cheaply the prevailing passenger demand. The reduced service level meant that the need to retain the LT stabling facilities at Croxley Green disappeared and the through service to Watford could no longer be justified. After several proposed withdrawal dates (all cancelled at short notice) the last timetabled Bakerloo Line train actually departed from Watford Junction on the morning of 24th September 1982. From this date Bakerloo trains were not scheduled to work north of Stonebridge Park.

Right **Poster announcing the withdrawal of Bakerloo Line trains to Watford which, since May 1966, had only run during the Monday to Friday peak hours – four journeys towards London in the morning and back to Watford in the evening.**

Below **One of the final 1938 Stock trains, in the 1971 corporate livery with white roundels, standing at Watford Junction.**

Facing page **Part of the 1983 Underground diagram, showing peak hour journeys only north of Queen's Park and BR service only north of Stonebridge Park.** LT Museum

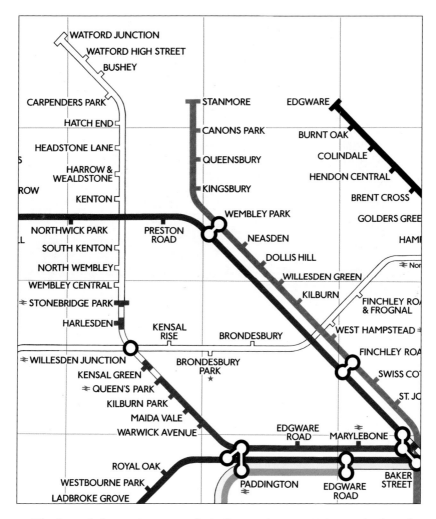

The loss of the service aroused significant adverse criticism and when the repercussions of the judicial decision had been finally settled, agreement was reached for a limited peak-hour service to be resumed as far as Harrow & Wealdstone, part of the costs being met by the Greater London Council. The 1974 London Rail Study had observed that the central London traffic from north of Queen's Park was split almost equally between BR and LT, though few LT passengers came from north of Harrow. A 15-minute peak hour service to Harrow, running in both directions during each peak period, resumed from 4th June 1984. The Bakerloo Line service south of Stonebridge Park was roughly at 7½-minute intervals.

The extended Bakerloo trains allowed British Rail to reduce the capacity of its own trains by introducing modern 3-car Class 313 multiple units of 1976 construction (displaced from the Eastern Region) in lieu of the 1957–59 origin 6-car trains which were withdrawn and scrapped.

Bakerloo Revitalised

Until about 1977 train services throughout the Bakerloo Line had continued to be provided by trains of 1938 Stock (at this time peak services in the central area were at 1½–2-minute intervals). The pre-1938 Stock trailers and the non-standard cars of 1949 origin had disappeared during the early 1970s when the fleet was rationalised, and trains were latterly all of standard formation. Many of the cars received a heavy overhaul from 1974 onwards, as it was considered that on the Bakerloo Line the stock would have a life extending into the 1980s. The obvious evidence of modification was the provision of 'outside door indicators', which came on when the doors on any car were open and stayed on if a door failed to close, making it quicker for staff to address the problem.

For the Fleet/Jubilee Line an interim order for new trains was made in 1972 in the form of thirty-three 7-car trains known as the 1972 Mark II Stock; these were initially put into service on the Northern Line to allow 1938 Stock to be scrapped. From 1977 they were gradually transferred to the Bakerloo where they operated alongside the 1938 Stock (some of which were scrapped), allowing staff to be trained and become familiar with the new trains. When the Jubilee Line opened in 1979 the 1972 Stock was retained on the Stanmore (Jubilee Line) service while the 1938 Stock became the mainstay of the truncated Bakerloo. As a concession to Bakerloo Line train staff that would otherwise have had to perform duty almost entirely in tunnel, both lines shared the same train staff pool for some years (about half the Jubilee Line mileage was in open air).

Through the early 1980s the 1938 Stock began to deteriorate rapidly and trains were reallocated to allow these veterans to be replaced. Small builds of stock elsewhere on the Underground, together with general service reductions, allowed 1959 Stock to be released from the Northern Line. The first 1959 Stock train entered service on the Bakerloo on 28th February 1983 and the last train of 1938 Stock was withdrawn on 20th November 1985. The 1959 Stock was a stop-gap, as the desire to convert the Bakerloo Line to one-person train operation required more modern trains. During summer 1986, some 14 trains of 1959 Stock were exchanged for a similar number of 1972 Mark II Stock trains (this was over 40 per cent of the Bakerloo's stockholding) to allow the technical work of conversion to begin.

Meanwhile a lull in the large-scale purchase of new Underground rolling stock allowed money to be diverted towards station refurbishments. Baker Street had already been improved, but the Jubilee Line was now showing up the Bakerloo Line platforms at Charing Cross as very old fashioned, and major refurbishment was authorised in 1981. What emerged in 1983 was strikingly different to the appearance of any other Bakerloo platform and consisted of white melamine panels on which were printed colour pictures based on paintings in the nearby National Gallery and National Portrait Gallery. The whole scheme benefited from additional, concealed lighting (a feature which would have brightened up the comparatively drab finishes at Baker Street). One of the more difficult jobs undertaken next was the refurbishment of the

Above **To facilitate reconstruction of a platform at Baker Street (Bakerloo), Stanmore branch trains were diverted to Baker Street (Metropolitan) station on three Sundays in summer 1977.** This very unusual expedient was augmented by buses between Baker Street and Finchley Road serving the intermediate stations. The picture shows a 1938 Stock train on platform 4. Brian Hardy

Left **An 'up' BR d.c. Watford to Euston train (of 1957–59 vintage) passing a Bakerloo Line train of 1959 Stock in the siding at Harrow & Wealdstone.**

Below **Kensal Green station with a refurbished 1972 Mk II Stock train.** Brian Hardy

Bright and attractive tiling at the modernised Piccadilly Circus station. Capital Transport

period ticket hall at Piccadilly Circus, restoring it to its 1920s splendour; the work was especially complicated in that the opportunity was taken to widen nearly all the access subways as part of the scheme. The work was completed in 1989 and subsequently allowed the closure of the Jermyn Street exit (the old station site was later incorporated into a property development).

By comparison with Charing Cross, platform refurbishments at Waterloo, Embankment, Piccadilly Circus, Oxford Circus and Paddington were more mundane, though bringing new tilework designs underground. Each had a different style. Paddington incorporated a motif based on an early tunnelling machine and the tiling at Oxford Circus was based on a maze pattern, redolent of people going up and down escalators.

By the early 1970s the Bakerloo's lifts and escalator fleet was getting quite old, which precipitated a massive programme of replacement and updating which continued throughout the 1980s. Except at Waterloo (Shell), Marylebone and those stations that became part of the Jubilee Line, many of the escalators on the Bakerloo Line had been of the 'L' type installed during the 1920s and were now about 50 years old. Progressively, each was withdrawn from service and totally refurbished, the resulting machines having much new running gear, with brushed steel panelling and metal treads instead of wooden components. At Embankment, Baker Street, Warwick Avenue, Maida Vale and Kilburn Park the original escalators of pre-1920 origin still existed, though these had been modernised and updated before the Second World War at which time the 'shunt' type landings had been replaced with the later standard type with cleated steps and combs. Even though refurbished they were now worn out again and so were progressively replaced, the programme being completed by 1988.

The Bakerloo Line had retained the original Otis lifts at Elephant & Castle, Lambeth North, Waterloo, Regent's Park and Edgware Road until comparatively recent times. The lifts at Waterloo had been withdrawn from service in March 1973, following the introduction (in 1970) of two additional escalators and an enlarged ticket hall, adjacent to the existing shaft, which came up beneath the main line station. At the remaining stations it was proposed to replace the existing lifts by new ones in the same shafts. At Regent's Park the decision was taken to withdraw the lift service completely from September 1984 while the existing lifts were replaced, the new ones coming into use in January 1987 (problems had arisen in replacing the lifts one at a time). Similarly, Lambeth North was without lifts while the old pair was replaced between June 1986 and February 1988.

Another scheme causing a considerable public impact was the huge project to install the new systemwide Underground Ticketing System (UTS), undertaken between the end of 1986 and 1990. This introduced one or more new, high security ticket offices at each station, each equipped with computerised ticket issuing equipment and passenger operated ticket machines that could be serviced from within the ticket office area. In central London (Zone 1), stations were equipped with automatic ticket gates to check all tickets on entry to and exit from the system. At other stations manual ticket checking was retained for the time being, supplemented by random checks on trains and at interchanges, reinforced by a penalty fares scheme applying to anyone found without a proper ticket.

A by-product of the new ticket system was that all the old-fashioned ticket offices were swept away. These included the free-standing booths known as 'Passimeters', the first of which was introduced at Kilburn Park station in 1921. Under the Passimeter

Below left **Interior of a 1972 MkII Stock non-driving motor car after refurbishment.**

Below right **Oxford Circus was one of several stations refurbished in the late 1980s. The heavy appearance of the continuous name frieze was the result of using it to conceal the ever-growing mass of station cabling, though it does cast a rather heavy shadow.**

system the original idea was that the booking clerk at quiet times not only issued tickets, but also checked tickets already held by inwards passengers, and checked or collected tickets of outwards passengers. This system became quite widespread in the 1920s and 1930s but largely fell into disuse after the war, although the booths remained for ticket issuing. The Passimeter system remained substantially intact at Warwick Avenue, Maida Vale and Kilburn Park until UTS arrived.

In the early 1980s it became known that the government proposed to abolish the GLC, and as a preparatory measure restructured London Transport once more as a nationalised industry reporting to the Secretary of State for Transport. The new body, known as London Regional Transport, came into existence on Friday 29th June 1984, just three days after the London Regional Transport Act received the royal assent. Under a provision of that Act a subsidiary company was established on 29th March 1985 called London Underground Limited and on 1st April 1985 London Regional Transport's railway interests passed to this subsidiary company, where they remain today.

The upswing in London's economy, together with the introduction of fare zones and the Travelcard were major factors in starting the continuing boom in passenger travel. Passenger journeys on the Underground rose by 50 per cent in the period 1981 to 1988, and very quickly brought about an urgent need for improved service frequencies and additional trains, for which LT were not entirely prepared (history having indicated a declining trend). New stock deliveries and train re-allocations allowed the remaining Bakerloo 1959 Stock to be returned to the Northern Line in exchange for further 1972 Mark II Stock, which, from early 1989, now provided the whole of the Bakerloo Line service. Following the necessary technical work during 1988/9 trains are all equipped for one-person operation (trains began operation without guards in November 1989).

LUL was not the only body benefiting from increased traffic. Government approval for joint LT/BR Capitalcards (now Travelcards) from January 1985 and the launch of 'Network SouthEast' in 1986 helped substantially to revive passenger business on BR-owned lines in the London area. The growth in demand led to pressure for resumption of through weekday off-peak trains from Harrow & Wealdstone to the Bakerloo Line, after their 20-year absence. These were finally re-introduced from 16th May 1988 at 20-minute intervals. LT Travelcard availability was extended to Harrow & Wealdstone at the same time (the more innovative LT tickets were not originally available on the BR section north of Queens Park). From 15th May 1989 a Sunday Bakerloo Line service was introduced to Harrow, at 30-minute intervals. Not all the news was good – from 2nd October 1989 BR reduced the Watford via Primrose Hill to the City service to a single train a day (with three more from Willesden) each way, and it wasn't long before these disappeared too.

In December 1988 the unique signalling system on the d.c. lines between Primrose Hill and Watford Junction was taken out of use and replaced with modern 2- or 3-aspect signals, power operated points and position-light shunt signals. Trackwork was largely unaltered but the emergency crossover at Kilburn High Road was moved to the north end of the station. New trainstops were provided on the section between Kilburn High Road and Harrow, over which Bakerloo Line trains operate (empty Bakerloo Line trains can reverse at Kilburn High Road). Earlier in the year one of the twin sidings at Harrow was removed and a new crossover was provided south of the station. North of Harrow nearly all the negative rail has been removed and there is little prospect of Bakerloo services resuming.

By the 1980s the existing signalling control on the LT-owned section was also becoming increasingly out-dated and modernisation works were put in hand. This was a two-stage process. First, new signalling and interlocking equipment had to be installed, in most cases controlled temporarily from panels in the existing signal cabins at the same or neighbouring locations. The process began at Paddington in June 1989 and took about two years. The second stage was the transfer of signalling control from the local sites to a new control centre at Baker Street; this was mainly undertaken in September 1991. Much of the automatic signalling was also updated during the same period.

During the 1980s the 1967 and 1972 stock (which included all the Bakerloo Line trains) was beginning to look distinctly scruffy. With another 20 years of life still left it was agreed to paint the exteriors and comprehensively refurbish the interiors, replacing potentially fire-hazardous materials at the same time. The contract for refurbishing the 1972 Mk II Stock trains was let to Tickford Rail Ltd in April 1990. The work was completed during 1995. During this time the fleet was augmented by a number of Mk I cars transferred from the Northern Line. Allowing for a slight reduction caused by collision damage, the Bakerloo is now allocated 37 trains.

The replacement of the last few Otis lifts of 1906 origin became urgent at around this time. Elephant & Castle was dealt with between 1987 and 1990, with a partial lift service maintained during the period (supplemented by the Northern Line's facilities). At Edgware Road it was felt necessary to close the station from December 1990 until January 1992 whilst this was done, creating a good opportunity to refurbish the platforms. These were finished in a modern interpretation of the original Yerkes style, a similar style of refurbishment also being employed at Marylebone, Lambeth North and Elephant & Castle. At Lambeth North and Regent's Park the stations remained open while the lifts were replaced.

Lambeth North after refurbishment in mock original style. Capital Transport

The wartime worries about the under-river tunnels rumbled on into the 1990s when it was decided to improve their integrity by encasing them in concrete reinforcement. The section south of Piccadilly Circus closed from 10th November 1996 until 14th July 1997 while this work was undertaken, although track improvements were also made. A closure such as this was an early example of a growing tendency for the Underground to close parts of the system to allow a concentration of works to take place rather than having partial closures over very much longer periods of time and at far greater cost.

Waterloo station, little changed since the 1950s, benefited from the arrival of the Eurostar terminal and the Jubilee Line. As part of these works the former cramped main ticket hall was greatly expanded and equipped with new entrances to deal with all the additional traffic; the enlarged ticket hall came into use in July 1994. Three new escalators led down to an additional lower concourse, later to lead to the extended Jubilee Line (which reached Waterloo in 1999).

In the years 1988–1999 service levels increased dramatically. In 1988 the maximum number of trains was increased from 25 to 27, then to 28 in 1992, 31 in 1995, and 32 in 1999. In 1987 scheduled central area frequencies were 3 minutes peak, 3½–4 minutes off-peak, 5 minutes Saturdays and 7½ minutes Sundays. In 1999 they had improved to 2½ minutes peak, 3 minutes off-peak and 3–3½ minutes Saturdays and Sundays. In 1987 services to Harrow operated at irregular intervals averaging about 12 minutes peak and 20 minutes off-peak and Saturdays. By 1999 they were running at about 10 minute intervals (and more regularly) for most of each day throughout the week.

The privatisation of Britain's railways in 1994 had little immediate impact on the Bakerloo Line, with the track north of Queen's Park passing to Railtrack plc and the stations and train services to North London Railways, now Silverlink; complex new legal agreements had to be put in place with LUL effectively becoming a train operating company buying timetable 'slots'. Silverlink continue to offer local services between Euston and Watford Junction at 20 minute intervals (30 minutes on Sundays) and also provide a similar number of semi fast services stopping at Watford Junction and Harrow & Wealdstone on the a.c. lines, with a proportion also stopping at Wembley Central and Queens Park. Railtrack have a programme to provide modest upgrading of all stations but during 1999 and early 2000 Stonebridge Park was (again) rebuilt and Willesden Junction received a new station building and access overbridge, replacing the old facilities at the north-west end of the platforms.

Train services on the Bakerloo are at a high, with trains recently refurbished. Reliability is good. The signalling is comparatively modern. All stations have been refurbished in recent years. And the Bakerloo Line is busy. In all probability the Bakerloo Line is now performing better than at any time. In essence it is the only one of the early 'tubes' to retain a comparatively simple service pattern over a comparatively short distance – the ideal arrangement for this type of railway. Of course the section north of Queen's Park presents operational complications and things are a little less than perfect, but here, too, equipment is more reliable than it has been for some time, the service pattern is simpler than in the past, and the run to Harrow nothing like as erratic as that to Watford was in later years. Extension to the south is still mooted occasionally, and there are some who view the Bakerloo as more fitted to the all stations Watford local services than a main line train operator. Time will tell which, if either scheme proceeds. In the meantime the Bakerloo remains in many ways very much the line opened in 1906–08, a great testament to the men of vision in those days, whatever their motives.